The World's Stupidest

CELEBRITIES

BARB KARG, RICK SUTHERLAND,
AND LUCIE CAVE

A adamsmedia
avon, massachusetts

Published by
Adams Media, an F+W Publications Company
57 Littlefield Street, Avon, MA 02322. U.S.A.
www.adamsmedia.com

Originally published by Michael O'Mara Books Ltd.
9 Lion Yard, Tremadoc Road
London SW4 7NQ
England

ISBN-10: 1-59869-595-9
ISBN-13: 978-1-59869-595-3

Printed in Canada

J I H G F E D C B A

Library of Congress Cataloging-in-Publication Data
is available from the publisher.

This publication is designed to provide accurate and authoritative
information with regard to the subject matter covered. It is sold
with the understanding that the publisher is not engaged in
rendering legal, accounting, or other professional advice. If legal
advice or other expert assistance is required, the services of a
competent professional person should be sought.
—From a *Declaration of Principles* jointly adopted by a Committee of the
American Bar Association and a Committee of Publishers and Associations

Many of the designations used by manufacturers and sellers
to distinguish their product are claimed as trademarks. Where
those designations appear in this book and Adams Media was
aware of a trademark claim, the designations have been printed
with initial capital letters.

This book is available at quantity discounts for bulk purchases.
For information, please call 1-800-289-0963.

This little jewel of pure inanity is dedicated to everyone on the planet who has ever done anything stupid.

You know who you are!

Acknowledgments

Writing and producing a book is never an easy endeavor and *The World's Stupidest Celebrities* is no exception to the rule. Thankfully, we're surrounded by a host of exceptional individuals who it is our privilege to know and to work with. For starters, we'd like to thank the fine folks at Adams Media with whom we've had the pleasure of working for many years. We offer our highest regards to director of innovation Paula Munier, a brilliant gal whose joie de vivre we appreciate and who we adore way more than cabernet and chocolate (and that's saying something!). We also salute Brendan O'Neill for his constant dedication, tenacity, and above all his sense of humor on each and every project. You guys are the best! As always, we also offer our sincere thanks to editorial director extraordinaire Laura Daly, copy chief Sheila Zwiebel, director of manufacturing Sue Beale, proofer Christine Beichner, and senior designer Colleen Cunningham for their tireless and exceptional work. You guys are a fabulous team and we greatly appreciate everything you do. On the home front, we forever have the unending support of our families and friends, all of whom we would be lost without. Our thanks to Ma, Pop, Dad, Chris, Glen, Anne, Terry, Kathy, the Blonde Bombshell, Ellen and Jim, Jeans and Jim, Karla, Jim V., Linda B., and the Scribe Tribe. You guys have all been a constant support and we consider your love and friendship one of the greatest gifts we could ever hope for. We love you all very much.

As usual, we'd like to give a special shout to Chris, Jeans, and Ellen for their dedication to finding all things stupid, and as always to Trudi Karg for plowing through our endless humorous rantings and keeping us on the straight and narrow. Thank you all for traveling with us on this journey of incessant blunder and buffoonery. And last, but certainly not least, we thank our flurry of four-legged children, Piper Maru, Jazz, Jinks, Maya, and Scout, who see us through thick and thin, keep us on our toes 24/7, and forever bring joy to our every waking moment. And our dear Sasha, Harley, and Mog who are always in our thoughts.

Many thanks to all of you!
Barb and Rick

Introduction

Celebrity (sa-le-bra-tee):

A famous person of prestige and class, whose name holds sway over the public, the nation, and the entire world.

Stupid Celebrity (stoopid sa-le-bra-tee):

A famous person who pulls some bonehead move or utters ridiculous statements that typically land them in court, in rehab, or on Letterman.

Love 'em or hate 'em, the world is teeming with celebrities who run the gamut from sweet and sublime to curious and baffling to outrageous and horrific. Over the millennia, entire nations and peoples have held high a dazzling array of talented scribes, poets, actors, politicians, and stunningly beautiful people. Unfortunately, the "beautiful people" among us have their fair share of scandalous encounters, sheer stupidity, and downright salacious behavior, none of which is unusual in the course of human events. Basically, celebrities are just like the rest of us, except they have tons more money, lots of exposure, and publicists made of solid steel.

Yet, stupidity lives on, and in fact flourishes amid a swirl of teen idols, wannabes, rehab heroes, and a slew of celebs who are old enough to know better. Gone are the carefree days of wine and roses. The days of Grace Kelly and Cary Grant, of Fred Astaire and Ginger Rogers. What we're left with are days of whining and implosions, and a host of inane celebs who are genetically predisposed to committing grandiose acts of stupidity, idiocy, travesty, intolerance, and an intergalactic black hole of demonic behavior. And that's just Paris Hilton.

In this classic little tome, you'll find a vast array of celebs, subject matter, jokes, quizzes, quotes, bumper stickers, and a shameful tour de farce of VIPs who have—intentionally or unintentionally—showcased their stupid actions, reactions, words, and bad behavior for all the world to see. No human ever wishes for a trainwreck to occur, but if one does, you can bet your last drop of Dom Perignon that we're all gonna watch the aftermath—

especially if someone famous is remotely involved.

Throughout this book you'll find juicy tid-bits like:

Stupid Says . . . • Stupid celeb quotes

Just Say Duh! • Stupid celeb blunders

Bumper Snickers • If celebs had them

Unholy Matrimony • Bad divorces

Wedded Miss • Shortest celeb weddings

He Said, She Said • Bad breakups

The Name Game • Hysterical celeb nicknames

They Said *What*? • Celebrity feuds

Jailbirds • Celebs in trouble with the law

Royal Blunders • Blueblood stupidity

Diva Darlings—Not! • Bad diva behavior

Say It Ain't So! • Products or organizations celebs should never endorse

Oh Baby! • Stupid celeb baby names

Leave a Message! • Celeb answering machines

On the Web • If celebs had Web sites

Nitwit Neuroses • Celeb phobias you don't wanna catch!

Pimp My Ride • Celeb vehicles

So join us as we enter a Twilight Zone of celebrity nonsense that's so ridiculous no one would dare make a Lifetime movie out of it. Enjoy!

We'll Always Have Paris . . . Unfortunately

There is perhaps no better way to begin a collection of inane celeb rantings than with Paris the heiress, the ultra-lithe dimwit who is famous for nothing other than having the last name Hilton. Love her or hate her, no one can deny that the slender word bender has the best publicist and lawyer that a *Simple Life* can buy. No doubt, you're dying to hear a few of her unending pearls of wisdom:

66If I could read a book, I'd definitely read one of yours.99 (to author Jackie Collins)

66What's Wal-Mart? Do they sell, like, wall stuff?99

66Like I really . . . I don't remember. I'm not like that smart.99

66It is like a weird Greek name. Like Douglas."

66People think I'm stupid. But I'm smarter than most people.99

66All British people have plain names, and that works pretty well over there.99

"There's nobody in the world like me. I think every decade has an iconic blonde—like Marilyn Monroe or Princess Diana—and right now, I'm that icon.**"**

Sorry, Paris honey, but you're no Lady Di. Harumpf!

Leave a Message!

Kim Basinger:
Kim here. I'm currently in hiding from my bully ex-husband. I'm armed and dangerous. And I'm PMSing. If this is my lawyer, page me.

Alec Baldwin:
Yo. You've reached Alec, victim of an unwarranted and ceaseless attack by the Wicked Witch of the West. I'm a sweet, loving father who adores his daughter with all his heart. You'll like me if you get to know me, especially since I finished my anger management program.

Ireland Baldwin:
Help!!!!

Viral VIPs

Match the celeb with their computer virus:

a. Ellen DeGeneres   **f.** Angelina Jolie
b. Britney Spears   **g.** Jerry Springer
c. Mel Gibson   **h.** Karl Rove
d. George W. Bush   **i.** Anna Nicole Smith
e. Nancy Kerrigan   **j.** Ronald Reagan

1. Every time you open a file it asks you if you remembered to wear underwear.
2. Your hard drive saves your files, but forgets where they're located.
3. Your Dell suddenly becomes a Macintosh.
4. In order to access your e-mail it asks for your DNA.
5. Every single e-mail you send or receive magically disappears without a trace.
6. All search functions fail because the drive has no weapons of mass destruction.
7. You can't access any programs unless you give a donation to UNICEF.
8. All of the menus are in Aramaic.
9. When you shut down it screams, "Why Why Why?!"
10. Every pop-up window accuses you of cheating with your brother's cousin's sister's aunt's Xbox.

Answers: 1-b, 2-j, 3-a, 4-i, 5-h, 6-d, 7-f, 8-c, 9-e, 10-g

HOW DOES MICHAEL JACKSON
PICK HIS NOSE?

FROM A CATALOG

Getting Juiced

He isn't much of an actor—at least not on the silver screen—but like a bad penny, the sheer madness that is O.J. Simpson just keeps turning up. It has been over a decade since his infamous murder trial, and still we are forced to suffer the blatant indignation of a guy who has done his best to keep the media frenzy firmly in the end zone. If it's not his quasi-confessional book *If I Did It* (which is now legally in the hands of the Goldman family), then it's trying to claim paternity over Anna Nicole Smith's baby. What's next? The semi-annual O.J. Simpson Ukrainian Midget Miniature Golf Tournament?

66When things have settled down a bit I will pursue as my primary goal in life the killer or killers who slaughtered Nicole and Mr. Goldman.99
—O.J. Simpson on the day of his acquittal in 1995

66It's a Bronco. It's what I drive, you know. I'd rather drive it than any other car.99

66The day you take complete responsibility for yourself, the day you stop making any excuses, that's the day you start to the top.99

66Everybody says they worry about my kids. But I would say this to America. You better hope your kids end up like my kid.99

66I really have reached a point where I can write a book about all of this.99

Stupid Says . . .

"I'm really into quantum physics. Some of my friends are into it, some of them aren't, so I'm trying to get them excited about discovering all these interesting things about thoughts and the power of thoughts. It gives me chills thinking about it. It's fun.**"**

—Carmen Electra

Unholy Matrimony

If you think your divorce was expensive, be glad you're not a celeb. According to *Forbes* magazine, the most expensive VIP divorce to date is the pending dissolution of hoopster Michael Jordan and his wife Juanita. During their eighteen years of wedded bliss Jordan raked in approximately $350 million. It is said that Juanita could walk away with over $150 million.

Just Say Duh!

Fergie, lead singer of the Black Eyed Peas, had a whizbanger of a time during a performance at San Diego's Street Scene Festival. Asked about her performance, Fergie claimed it was a tightly run venue—so tight that she had no time for a potty break. So, with all avenues blocked, the songbird "accidentally" tinkled on stage. It's safe to assume we should all be thankful she didn't eat Taco Bell for breakfast.

Bumper Snickers!

YOUR RIDICULOUS LITTLE OPINION
HAS BEEN NOTED.
Martha Stewart

HONK IF YOU'VE NEVER SEEN AN UZI
FIRED OUT THE BACK OF A CAR WINDOW.
Snoop Dogg

Nitwit Neuroses

Wackojackophobia:
Fear of having your nose fall off

Hiltophobia:
Fear of having to stay at a Motel 6

Fleissophobia:
Fear of dying and reincarnating at
the Mustang Ranch

Bushaphobia:
Irrational fear that your toilet is
a weapon of mass destruction

The Name Game

Forget Brangelina and Bennifer. Just think
of all the potential pet names the tabloids
could've given celebs if they'd hooked up.

Halle Berry and Richard Burton =
Halliburton

Sandra Oh and Boy George = OhBoy

Simon Cowell and Tipper Gore = CowTipper

Bea Arthur and Sting = BeaSting

Oops, She'll Do It Again!

The public follows Britney Spears' manhunts closer than they do the FBI's Top Ten Most Wanted criminals. Unfortunately, the infamous pop tart doesn't have the greatest track record. In an effort to escape dense partners, it is hoped that in the future she asks potential mates a few crucial questions:

- Are you or have you ever worked for Fed-Ex?
- Have you ever been a Mouseketeer?
- When you hear the word "rap," do you think of Eminem or Christmas paper?
- How do you feel about Sinead O'Connor?
- Are you opposed to mirrored ceilings?
- I'm willing to offer you a $40 prenup, are you okay with that?
- Are you good at buckling in car seats?
- Madonna's a great kisser, how about you?
- I don't do windows, diapers, dishes, underwear, or joint custody, can you handle all that?
- How many nights a week do you attend strip clubs?

WHAT'S THE DIFFERENCE BETWEEN NAOMI CAMPBELL PMSING **AND A PIT BULL?**

LIPSTICK

Diva Darlings—Not!

These days, most superstars have very specific requirements for their backstage hangouts, and a six-pack of Coke and a bucket of daisies simply won't do. Modern-day divas have contracts a mile long with a list of demands that cover everything from tofu to toilet paper. Among Beyonce Knowles many requirements is a 78 degree dressing room, a minimum of four brand new white towels, heavily seasoned juicy baked chicken, and a bathroom that's fully stocked and "cleaned with disinfectant and anti-bacteria products before she arrives." No doubt, lightening will strike if there's a ring around the tub!

Bumper Snickers!

WE ARE MICROSOFT. RESISTANCE IS FUTILE. YOU WILL BE ASSIMILATED.
Bill Gates

I'M NOT AN ALCOHOLIC. ALCOHOLICS GO TO MEETINGS. I AM A DRUNK.
Mel Gibson

On the Web

If dimwitted celebs had Web sites what would they be?

Britney Spears
www.igocommando.com

Tom Cruise
www.couchoffender.com

David Hasselhoff
www.legendinmyownmind.com

Winona Ryder
www.ihadthereceipts.com

Say It Ain't So!

Products or organizations that celebs should never endorse:

O.J. for Henkel Knives (or Ford Broncos)

Naomi Campbell for Blackberries

Paris Hilton for Blockbuster

Britney Spears for Hanes

Mix and Mingle: Annoying Celeb Anagrams

Alec Baldwin   Tom Cruise
Lindsay Lohan   Mel Gibson
Martha Stewart   Britney Spears
Donald Trump   Jessica Simpson
Mariah Carey   Paris Hilton

1. MICE TOURS
2. RATBEERS SPINY
3. BIG LEMONS
4. SPACE JOINS MISS
5. DAHLIA NYLONS
6. RANT ODDLUMP
7. A HIP NOSTRIL
8. ARMCHAIR AYE
9. BAD CLAWLINE
10. HAREM TARTWAST

Answers:
1-Tom Cruise.
2-Britney Spears.
3-Mel Gibson.
4-Jessica Simpson.
5-Lindsay Lohan.
6-Donald Trump.
7-Paris Hilton.
8-Mariah Carey.
9-Alec Baldwin.
10-Martha Stewart.

The Golden Schnozz Award

Sometimes you just gotta leave well enough alone, but in Tinseltown temptation is the foible of every starlet. Such was the case with actress Jennifer Grey, who catapulted to fame in 1987 as the adorable and endearing "Baby" in the cult classic *Dirty Dancing*. Five years later, Grey, daughter of renowned actor Joel Grey, crossed into the dark side of rhinoplasty. Two operations later Grey's nose looked great, but it also changed her appearance to such an extent that no one recognized her. Are you listening Joan Rivers?

Stupid Says . . .

❝Is this chicken or is this fish? I know it's tuna but it says Chicken of the Sea.**❞**
—Jessica Simpson

WHAT DID
HALEY JOEL OSMENT SAY WHEN HE GOT TO THE TOP OF MT. EVEREST?

"ICY DEAD PEOPLE"

Wedded Miss!

When it comes to short weddings there are more than a few celebs who stupidly took the plunge and then swam like hell to get out of the pool. Drew Barrymore's marriage to Jeremy Thomas lasted a mere four weeks in 1994, followed by a whopping five-month hitching in 2001 to questionable comic Tom Green. Terminally bad girl Shannen Doherty wasn't charmed by first husband Ashley Hamilton (George Hamilton's son), to whom she was married for five months. Nor was she bewitched by her nine-month marriage to Rick Salomon, a sterling character who later wreaked havoc on planet Earth by starring in a sex tape with Paris Hilton in 2003—and then in 2007 married Pamela Anderson.

Deep Thoughts

If Donald Trump was caught soliciting, would he be called Donald Tramp?

Stupid Says . . .

66Whenever I watch TV and see those poor starving kids all over the world, I can't help but cry. I mean I'd love to be skinny like that but not with all those flies and death and stuff.99

—Mariah Carey

Oh Baby!

When it comes to naming their children, more than a few dimwitted celebs have bestowed upon their progeny the most ridiculous names known to mankind. If you thought Frank Zappa was a bit off naming his kids Moon Unit, Dweezil, Ahmet Emuukha Rodan, and Diva Thin Muffin Pigeen, then hold on to your hats. Comedian Penn Jillette named his daughter Moxie Crimefighter and his son Zolten. Not to be outdone, actress Shannyn Sossamon named her son Audio Science. Who names a kid Audio Science?

WHAT'S THE DIFFERENCE BETWEEN

BIGFOOT

AND AN INTELLIGENT

CELEBRITY?

BIGFOOT HAS ACTUALLY

BEEN SPOTTED

SEVERAL

T I M E S

Royal Blunders

It was a sad day indeed in the United Kingdom when Lady Di's precious Prince Harry made a royal faux pas of biblical proportion. It seems the little prince who might be king showed up to a 2005 fancy dress party wearing an SS uniform complete with swastika armband. Dubbed "Harry the Nazi" by *The Sun* newspaper, Harry's royal gaffe caused quite a public ruckus. Apology notwithstanding, Harry's misplaced attempt at humor became part of a long line of royal mishaps.

Celebrity Pit Stops

What do Julia Roberts and Drew Barrymore have in common? Here's a hint: It has nothing to do with acting and everything to do with their personal shaving habits. If you guessed hairy armpits, you would be correct. Never have pits received so much ill notoriety since the red carpet premiere of *Troy*. The pretty woman created a major media twizzle back in 1999 when her hairy pits overshadowed her waving to a red carpet crowd at the *Notting Hill* premiere in Britain. Barrymore likewise exhibited her liberated pits on the catwalk at a Marc Jacobs show in New York. Hasn't anyone heard of Nair?

Nitwit Neuroses

Vannaphobia:
Fear of vowels

Springerphobia:
Fear of your brother's mother's sister's
ex-husband's great uncle

Geraldophobia:
Fear of tabloid journalism

Biggiesmallaphobia:
Fear of supersized meals

Jailbirds

July 28, 2006 was a sucky day for A-list celeb
Mel Gibson when he was arrested for drunk
driving in Malibu, California. Bad enough
his blood alcohol level was well over the
legal limit, worse was the anti-Semitic rant
that Really Mad Max unleashed when officers arrested him. Gibson's dispassionate
lunatic ravings shocked the world and
brought his career to a grinding halt. Once
sober, the Academy Award-winning director
put up a brave heart and apologized to the
world for his belligerence, as well as revealing his long-time battle with alcoholism.

Bumper Snickers!

> HONK IF ANYTHING FALLS OFF.
> Michael Jackson

> WHAT IF THE HOKEY POKEY IS WHAT IT'S REALLY ALL ABOUT?
> George W. Bush

The Name Game

If these celebs had gotten together!

Courtney Love and Shaquille O'Neal = Loveshack

Cindy Crawford and P. Diddy = Crawdiddy

Linda Bloodworth and Al Gore = BloodnGore

Demi Moore, P. Diddy, and Jennifer Love Hewitt = MoDiddyLove

Top Ten Ways to Drive Martha Stewart Insane

1. Sneak into her kitchen in the middle of the night and rearrange her alphabetized spice rack.
2. Serve her CheezWhiz and Chicken 'n a Biscuit.
3. Inform her that your egg-laying hens are on vacation, and the poached eggs you've just served her are store bought.
4. Put iodized salt in her salt shaker.
5. Tell her that Williams-Sonoma refused to close their store for a private shopping spree.
6. Mention that you'd rather sleep on a bed of nails than buy her gingham sheets from Kmart.
7. Deprive her of foie gras and Dom Perignon for an entire week.
8. Throw a surprise party for her and invite all the parolees from Alderson Federal Prison Camp.
9. Strand her on a deserted island in the Bermuda Triangle with Donald Trump.
10. Send her an ankle bracelet for Christmas.

Favorite Movies of the Truly Daft

Pamela Anderson:
Brokeback Mountains

Britney Spears:
Of Mouseketeers and Men

Mel Gibson:
I Walk the Line

Bill Gates:
Rear Windows XP

Leave a Message!

Tom Cruise:
This is Tom. I can't come to the phone right now, I'm currently out saving the female population from postpartum depression. Leave your address and I'll send you a case of multi-vitamins. This answering machine will self-destruct in thirty seconds.

Family Ties

Renowned director and comic genius Woody Allen wasn't laughing when longtime love Mia Farrow found photographs of her twenty-one-year-old daughter Soon-Yi Previn in Allen's New York flat in 1992. Had they been family pics, there wouldn't have been a problem. However, Soon-Yi was au naturel and Allen, thirty-five years her senior, was in for the fight of his life. What followed was a sordid and very public custody battle with accusations of abuse and moral questions regarding his and Soon-Yi's relationship. Farrow won the court battle. In 1997, Allen married Soon-Yi and they eventually adopted daughters Bechet and Manzie. And you thought your family was dysfunctional?

Stupid Says . . .

66Smoking kills. If you're killed, you've lost an important part of your life.99
—Brooke Shields

He Said, She Said

Breaking up is always hard to do, especially if both parties are high profile and particularly volatile. Such was the case with James Woods and Sean Young, who began dating during the filming of their 1988 movie *The Boost*. Unfortunately, the pairing of Woods and Young was as stable as a Russian nuclear reactor. In 1989, Young was sued for harassment, with Woods claiming his former paramour had gone all *Fatal Attraction* on him and was destroying his property and sending images of dead things. His then-fiancée Sarah Owen was also in the mix. Branded a wacknut, Young's reputation suffered despite the fact that Woods dropped the suit and it was allegedly settled out of court for a figure as high as a quarter million dollars. Woods' subsequent marriage to Owen lasted only a few months, with Owen accusing him of a host of abuses and lewd behavior that occurred both before and after their marriage. He allegedly nicknamed Owen "the anti-Christ." What a charmer.

The 2007 Nudie Award

Let it be said that there's nothing wrong with the human body, but there's definitely a time and place for going au naturel—especially if you're a pop princess. Apparently it's of little concern to ingénue Christina Aguilera and her husband of one year, Jordan Bratman. In February 2007, during a stint on *Ellen*, the *Stripped* singer announced that she and her hubby have a tradition called "naked Sundays." And yes, it's what it sounds like. They spend the entire day at home in the buff, lounging about and cooking up a storm. Does that sound like an open invitation for the paparazzi to start hiding in the Bratmans' bushes?

Leave a Message!

Russell Crowe:
G'day mate. Obviously I'm out bashing the bricks with my boys. Love to chat with you, but I'm still in phone rehab. Technically, I'm not allowed to be within 100 feet of anything you can bloody well dial. So drop me a postcard and I'll get back to you.

The Name Game

If these celebs had gotten together!

Deborah Harry and Mandy Patinkin = HarryMan

Paris Hilton and Peter Boyle = Parboil

David Hasselhoff and Matt LeBlanc = Hasmat

Moon Unit Zappa and Snoop Dog = MoonDoggie

Unholy Matrimony

Ranked number two on *Forbes* 2007 list of most expensive divorces is singer Neil Diamond and his wife Marcia Murphey. Married in 1969, they divorced in 1996, with Marcia singing to the tune of approximately $150 million. Of the divorce, Diamond purportedly said that his former wife was "worth every penny."

Note to Mr. Diamond: She was your partner, Mr. You-Don't-Bring-Me-Flowers—not a condo complex in Maui!

Wedded Miss

Lisa Marie Presley has had her fair share of strife living in the public eye, but the King's daughter has perhaps never been more persecuted than when she married Wacko Jacko. In 1994, Elvis' pride and joy married the King of Pop much to the utter shock of the entire world. In a grand effort to justify such a pairing, some surmised that the two had a lot in common, having grown up under close public scrutiny. Wrong! Less than two years later, Lisa Marie and Michael Jackson divorced. Presley later endured an equally baffling three-month marriage to Nicholas Cage, and then married yet another bloke in 2006. Jackson continued to wage his fight for normalcy. Results of his fight are as yet unknown.

Favorite Movies of the Truly Daft

Rosie O'Donnell:
The Twin Towering Infernos

Donald Trump:
It's a Wonderful Wife

Nicole Ritchie:
Ben Hurl

Rush Limbaugh:
In the Bleat of the Night

WHAT WAS SO GOOD
ABOUT THE
NEUROTIC DOLL
DINA LOHAN GAVE DAUGHTER
LINDSAY
FOR   CHRISTMAS?

IT WAS ALREADY
WOUND UP

Foot in Mouth Award

There are only a small handful of elite actors who are lucky enough to maintain a role on a hit television drama. Isaiah Washington is such an actor, having landed the plum roll of Dr. Preston Xavier Burke on the ABC megahit *Grey's Anatomy*. But by October 2006 all was not well in the ER, when Washington was allegedly involved in an on-set altercation with McDreamy co-star Patrick Dempsey over a slur directed at castmate T.R. Knight, who ultimately was forced out of the closet. Backstage at the 2007 Golden Globe Awards all hell broke loose when, after winning the Globe for Best Drama, Washington repeated his slur for all to hear while attempting to explain the previous conflict. After rounds of apologies, Washington ended up in counseling and facing an uncertain acting future. By June 2007, Washington was fired from *Grey's Anatomy*—one of the top-rated shows on television. Open mouth, insert foot.

Grey Matter

Not so lucky celebs who were turned down for roles on Grey's Anatomy:

- McSneezy: Keith Richards
- McEasy: George Michael
- McCrazy: Ray Liotta
- McLazy: Bobby Brown
- McCheesy: Donald Trump
- McQueasy: Marilyn Manson
- McSleazy: Pee Wee Herman
- McTeasy: David Spade
- McMeany: Russell Crowe
- McBeatit: Michael Jackson

Pimp My Ride

Mel Gibson:
Honda Discord

Tom Sizemore:
VW Thug

Mariah Carey:
Chrysler LeBareall

George W. Bush:
Pontiac Bonnevillain

Bumper Snickers!

FRIENDS HELP YOU MOVE. REAL
FRIENDS HELP YOU MOVE BODIES.
O.J. Simpson

WHERE THERE'S A WILL,
I WANT TO BE IN IT!
Anna Nicole Smith

Royal Blunders

During a presentation of the Duke of Edinburgh Award, historically provided to young people in the British Commonwealth for personal achievement, Prince Philip was informed that the young student receiving the award was going to Romania to help out. Philip inquired if the young man was going to be working with Romanian orphans. Upon hearing that the recipient was not, the Prince said, "Ah good, there's so many over there, you feel they breed them just to put them in orphanages."

Oh Baby!

Our celeb cousins across the pond have come up with a handful of intriguing names, none of which any of us has probably ever heard of. Designer Anna Ryder-Richardson of *Changing Rooms* fame named her twin daughters Dixie Dot and Bibi Belle. Naked Chef Jamie Oliver's two buns popped out of the oven and were dubbed Poppy Honey and Daisy Boo. Not to be outdone was Live Aid creator Bob Geldof whose trio of gals is known as Fifi Trixibell, Little Pixie, and Peaches Honeyblossom. At least they didn't settle for Victoria, Elizabeth, or Fergie.

Stupid Says . . .

(I hope) my child will be a good Catholic like me.

—Madonna

Just Say Duh!

April 21, 1986 was a day that will live in television infamy. It was the day that the entire American nation—every man, woman, and child—got suckered into watching *The Mystery of Al Capone's Vault*. Yes. We all got suckered, and we have Geraldo Rivera to blame for all eternity. For two painful hours, we wasted our lives, our eyes glued to the mega-hyped spectacle that was to uncover a time capsule of items, astounding wealth, or even show us where the bodies were buried. Over thirty million people held their breath as Geraldo opened the vault and found . . . nothing. Zip. Nada. Nothing but dirt and a few empty bottles. The show had the highest-ever ratings in television history for a live syndicated special. And we got dirt.

For shame Geraldo . . . for shame.

Deep Thoughts

If Madonna bought an airline, would it be called "Like a Virgin" Air?

Top Ten Ways to Drive Tom Cruise Insane

1. Tell him Scientology is Mission Impossible.
2. Send him thousands of autographed copies of Brooke Shield's book *Down Came the Rain*.
3. Tell him that your top gun is bigger than his.
4. Remind him that he's no Bela Lugosi.
5. When he moves toward your couch start screaming, "For the love of God, nooooooo!"
6. Let him know that his Oscar nomination for *The Last Samurai* is still lost in the mail.
7. Ask if his wife is related to porn king John Holmes.
8. Tell him that he needs to get his head examined.
9. Ask him if the third time's the charm.
10. Inform him that his time is up. The mothership has come back to retrieve him.

They Said *What?*

It should come as no surprise to anyone that Zsa Zsa Gabor has been involved in more than a few scandals, spats, and court cases. But one feud in particular cost her big bucks. In a 1993 suit brought on by actress Elke Sommer, Gabor was sued for libel. The story goes that Sommer initially commented that Gabor had a rather large caboose, to which Gabor publicly responded that Sommer's career was "washed up." Then Zsa Zsa's Austrian hubby, faux Prince Frederic von Anhalt, stepped in and it all went to hell. He alleged that Sommer said, "All German men are pigs." (Don't you love it when blondes bicker?) Off to court they went, and when they reemerged, Gabor was ordered to pay Sommer approximately $1.25 million in damages. Sommer got the last laugh, and Gabor had to declare bankruptcy. How tragic, dahlink!

HOW MANY CELEBRITY
LAWYERS
DOES IT TAKE TO
SCREW
IN A LIGHT BULB?

TWO. ONE TO DECLARE IT'S
DEFECTIVE
AND THE OTHER TO ACQUIT IT

Clueless Wonders

Questions that simpleminded celebs
don't understand:

Question: When you go to the store
can you pick up some carrots?

Answer: I'm not going to Harry Winston's.

Nitwit Neuroses

Madmaxophobia:
Fear of destroying your career

Jessophobia:
Fear of Daisy Dukes

Affleckophobia:
Fear of ducks

Marthaphobia:
Fear of Kmart

Viral VIPs

Match the celeb with their computer virus.

a. David Cassidy   **e.** Whitney Houston
b. Geraldo Rivera   **f.** Johnnie Cochran
c. Sally Field   **g.** Martha Stewart
d. Cartman   **h.** Mariah Carey

1. When you boot up, your hard drive starts whining in several octaves.

2. When you try to run disk first aid it says: Screw you guys, I'm going home.

3. Upon exiting a program it asks if you want to acquit.

4. Every time you insert a page it starts screaming "Crack is whack! Crack is whack!"

5. All of your folders are marked Al Capone's Vault.

6. Whenever you save a file it starts crying: You like me. You really like me!!

7. If you attempt to do a Google search it asks you to sing "I Think I Love You."

8. If your machine freezes a message informs you that your napkin rings don't match, your duck a l'orange sucks, and the flower boxes you hand-painted look like headstones.

Answers:
1-h, 2-d,
3-f, 4-e, 5-b,
6-c, 7-a,
8-g.

Unholy Matrimony

For many years, Stephen Spielberg topped the list of *Forbes* most costly divorces, so it's a safe bet that he's happy to give up the number one spot. Now coming in third on the list is Spielberg's first attempt at wedded bliss gone amiss with actress Amy Irving. Their four-year communing from 1984 to 1989 gave Irving a whopping $100 million as a result of a prenuptial agreement that was overturned, given that it was allegedly written on a napkin! Of course, that's chump change considering *E.T.*'s benefactor has a current estimated worth of over three billion. Now that's something to phone home about.

Stupid Says . . .

❝There's a sculpture in our bedroom, a solid brass replica of Antonio's manhood. It's very expensive, he gave it to me as a romantic gift.**❞**

—Melanie Griffith

Say It Ain't So!

Products or organizations that celebs should never endorse:

Snoop Dog for Smith and Wesson

Tom Cruise for La-Z-Boy

Wesley Snipes for H&R Block

Gwyneth Paltrow for Kentucky Fried Chicken

Diva Darlings—Not!

On our birthdays most of us mere mortals enjoy a store-bought birthday cake. If we're really lucky, we get a homemade cake. On her thirty-fifth birthday in 2005, Mariah Carey decided that she needed a life-size replica of herself made out of cake. At a cost of $9,500, the six-foot tall sponge cake, which was filled with praline butter cream, was made by seventeen chefs from London's famed Harrods store. For those who are counting, the price of that cake was more than the entire ticket sales of Carey's über-flop, *Glitter*.

Who's Your Daddy?

The tragic death of covergirl Anna Nicole Smith on February 8, 2007 began yet another category five hurricane of controversy that will no doubt remain in the judicial system for years. The current trouble began with the birth of Smith's daughter, Dannielynn, on September 7, 2006, and the death of her twenty-year-old son Daniel three days later in Smith's hospital room. While Daniel's death awaited a Bahamian inquest, all eyes turned to the question of baby Dannielynn.

Smith's longtime lawyer and companion Howard K. Stern was named father on the birth certificate, but ex-boyfriend and photographer Larry Birkhead filed a paternity suit. Immediately after Smith's death, a pack of rabid wannabe dads lined up to claim heritage of the potential half-billion dollar baby. These included Zsa Zsa Gabor's hubby Prince Frederic von Anhalt, Smith's former bodyguard Alexander Denk, ex-boyfriend and current convict Mark Hatten, and shamefully, a typically media hungry O.J. Simpson. After months of court play, Birkhead eventually came out on top of the daddy database.

Bottom's Up!

If name dropping were a drinking game, we'd all be three sheets to the wind. No doubt this mouthful would prove lethal if every time you heard the word "Bobby" you had to face a beer bong and a tequila chaser:

❝You can expect Bobby to be Bobby. If Bobby ain't Bobby, Bobby just can't be Bobby.❞
—Bobby Brown

And just in case that wasn't confusing enough, add to the mix Brown's then-wife, songbird and professional diva Whitney Houston, who in a 2002 interview famously told *Primetime's* Diane Sawyer:

❝Let's get one thing straight. Crack is cheap. I make too much money to ever smoke crack. Let's get that straight. Crack is whack.❞

And you wonder what life was like in *that* household?

On the Web

Jessica Simpson
www.putupyourdaisydukes.com

O.J. Simpson
www.slashslashslash.com

Pamela Anderson
www.iheartsilicone.org

Donald Trump
www.sexycombover.com

Nitwit Neuroses

Trebekophobia:
Fear of questions

Pennophobia:
Fear of Madonna

Katieholmaphobia:
Fear of *Stepford Wives*

Snoopdogaphobia:
Fear of firearms

Just Say Duh!

There are few people on the planet who haven't heard of or watched even a snippet of the show *Baywatch*. But like it or not, it's one of the most popular shows in the world, presumably for its quintessential storylines and character development. David Hasselhoff perhaps said it best:

❝Beyond its entertainment value, Baywatch has enriched and, in many cases, helped save lives. I'm looking forward to the opportunity to continue with a project which has had such a significance for so many.❞

Wow. Who knew? Apparently not Jessica Simpson. The gal who can't distinguish canned tuna from chicken, once asked *Baywatch* babe Pamela Anderson a question of utmost importance:

❝How did you guys run so slowly in the show's opening scene? You know, where you're running down the beach?❞

Apparently that statement even rendered Anderson speechless. After the coma wore off, the former *Baywatch* babe allegedly had to explain to her fellow blondette that the sequences were filmed in slow motion. Ha! Once again, it's proven that millions of bucks can't buy a higher intelligent quotient.

The Name Game

If these celebs had gotten together!

James Coburn and Slash = SlashnBurn

Helena Bonham Carter and Jack Nicholson = CarJack

Ty Pennington and David Bowie = BowTy

Gunnar Nelson and Rosie O'Donnell = GunsnRoses

Favorite Movies of the Truly Daft

Rupaul: The Drag Queen

Anna Nicole Smith: Something's Gotta Live

Dan Quayle: Pulp Diction

Hillary Clinton: Kill Bill (Vols. 1 and 2)

Three Strikes and Yer Out!

It's all too common to read stories about men beating up women, but what isn't common is a woman roughing up a dude. Redheaded eighties bombshell Tawny Kitaen singled herself out in 2002 when she attacked husband Chuck Finley, a pitcher for the Cleveland Indians. It should be noted that Finley is six-foot-six and weighed over 230 pounds at the time, and that Brawny Tawny made short work of him by kicking him with her high heel. He filed for divorce, and she spent a few days in the pokey after which charges were dropped pending her agreeing to counseling. Of course it didn't end there for the former Whitesnake video maven. In 2006, she was busted for cocaine possession, and again escaped serious jail time by doing a stint in rehab. Who knew that a gal whose career began by co-starring with Tom Hanks in *Bachelor Party* could become such a menace?

Deep Thoughts

If Britney created a line of scissors, would
they be called Britney Shears?

Stupid Says . . .

66The soundtrack to Indecent Exposure is
a romantic mix of music that I know most
women love to hear, so I never keep it far
from me when women are nearby.99

—Fabio

A Star Is Shorn

There once was a pop tart named Brit
Whose underwear didn't quite fit
So she tossed it aside
And got out of her ride
To become this year's rehabbing twit!

Bumper Snickers

SAVE YOUR BREATH. YOU'LL NEED
IT TO BLOW UP YOUR DATE.
Jenna Jameson

ALCOHOL AND CALCULUS DON'T MIX.
NEVER DRINK AND DERIVE.
Albert Einstein

Leave a Message!

Victoria "Posh" Beckham:
You've reached Posh Spice. I'm too busy to take your call. I ate a grape this morning and it'll take me the rest of the day to work it off. If you're a realtor and you've found us a home in Bel Air in the $75 million range leave a number and we'll ring you—but only if the mansion has a minimum of forty-eight loos and a heated helipad.

Match the celeb with their idiotic behavior:

a. Denise Richards   **f.** Britney Spears
b. Farrah Fawcett   **g.** Russell Crowe
c. Virgie Arthur   **h.** George Michael
d. Keith Richards   **i.** Naomi Campbell
e. Tom Cruise   **j.** Hugh Grant

1. Got caught with his pants down in a public restroom.
2. Left home without her underwear and turned "commando" into something not involving a mercenary.
3. Hucked a phone at a hotel concierge.
4. Got picked up twice for shoplifting.
5. Lashed out on *The Early Show* about the evils of psychiatry.
6. Tossed jewel encrusted Blackberries at her assistants.
7. Got picked up for soliciting a prostitute.
8. Dropped a laptop off a hotel balcony and barely missed two innocent bystanders.
9. Joked that he snorted his father's ashes with cocaine.
10. Tried to legally halt her daughter's funeral as the hearse was waiting in front of the church.

Answers:
1-h, 2-f, 3-g,
4-b, 5-e, 6-
i, 7-j, 8-a,
9-d, 10-c

Decline of the British Empire

66We are not interested in the possibilities of defeat.99

—Queen Victoria, 1899

66How's the Empire?99

—King George, 1936

66I want to be reincarnated as your tampon.99
—Prince Charles to
Camilla Parker Bowles in 1991

Pimp My Ride

Naomi Campbell:
Cruella DeVille

Rush Limbaugh:
Dodge Intrepig

Dick Cheney:
Yukon Svengali

Tonya Harding:
PT Bruiser

DID YOU KNOW CAPTAIN KIRK HAD THREE EARS?

HIS LEFT EAR, HIS RIGHT EAR AND **HIS FINAL** FRONTIER

Royal Blunders

Prince Charles wrote a memo in 2003 that included a number of scathing comments about the aspirations and abilities of England's common folk. Among the crown jewels in his missive were observations that the United Kingdom's "learning culture" gave people hope beyond their capabilities, and asked the question, "What is it that makes everyone seem to think they are qualified to do things far beyond their technical abilities?"

The Prince continued by deriding a "child-centered system" which leads people to believe that they can achieve greatness without "putting in the necessary effort or having the natural abilities." Taken out of context, the Prince's comments seem unnecessarily harsh and dismissive of the general population. On the flip side, taken in context, the Prince's comments seem remarkably similar.

The Prince finished by noting that, "I hardly dare say anything. I don't really want to teach any more grandmothers to suck eggs." Which is a metaphorical way of insinuating that if people are too stupid to understand what he's saying, there's no point in explaining it. The Prince declined the opportunity to clarify his remarks.

If the Brain Don't Fit . . .

Part-time media monger and alleged maniac O.J. Simpson is always embroiled in controversy. It wasn't bad enough that he wrote *If I Did It* (which got shelved then subsequently went up for auction and publication). In March 2007, in true narcissistic fashion, the Juice couldn't help but inject himself into the now legendary Anna Nicole Smith paternity battle. Simpson even managed to merge the two horrific events by claiming that he could be the father of Dannielynn Hope Marshall Stern as a result of "slow moving sperm," but that he didn't want to know because if he was the father he didn't want Fred Goldman "trying to seize her money or the baby herself." Keep in mind that Smith and Simpson filmed the *Naked Gun 33⅓: The Final Insult* together in 1994, making his sperm the slowest moving in history. Ladies and gentlemen, there is no end to the insanity that is O.J. Simpson.

The 2007 Yul Brynner Award

Let it be duly noted that this year's recipient of the Yul Brynner Award is undisputed. February 17, 2007, is a day that shall live in infamy, as it marks a "mane" event in pop music's long and often tumultuous history. It was the day that Britney Spears became Britney Shears, and who before God and hordes of paparazzi picked up an electric razor and decided to go Manson on us. Following the meltdown were a pair of tattoos, three attempts at rehab, a nominal million-dollar payoff to her ex, K-Fed, and a custody battle.

Deep Thoughts

If Halle Berry purchased a fleet of commuter vessels, would they be called Halle Ferrys?

Stupid Says . . .

❝You know, one of the hardest parts of my job is to connect Iraq to the war on terror.❞

—George W. Bush

Foot in Mouth Award

Actor Jon Voight has always been a bit of an enigma, but during a 2002 interview with *E! News Live* the former *Midnight Cowboy* got himself into a whole heap o' trouble with megastar daughter Angelina Jolie. At the time, Jolie's eccentric marriage to Billy Bob Thornton was in the dumper, and Voight, who had progressively lost contact with her since they co-starred in the 2000 film *Lara Croft: Tomb Raider,* was overtaken by the urge to sobbingly tell the world that she was suffering from "serious emotional problems." Jolie, whose father was absent during her childhood after divorcing her mother Marcheline Bertrand while Jolie was still a baby, made public that "it is not healthy for me to be around my father." As of 2007, Voight still hadn't spoken to his charity-loving progeny or any of his grandchildren. Coming home, it would seem, remains elusive for the uber-blubbering Oscar winner.

HOW MANY STUPID
C E L E B S
DOES IT TAKE TO MAKE
POPCORN?

THREE. ONE TO HOLD
THE PAN.
TWO TO SHAKE
THE STOVE

The Name Game

If these celebs had gotten together!

Bea Arthur and Tori Spelling = SpellingBea

Madonna and Scooter Libby = MadLib

Liv Tyler and Alec Baldwin = LivBald

Carmen Electra and Isaiah Washington =
CarWash

Wedded Miss

They were dubbed "beauty and the beast,"
and they never lived it down. The surprise
hitching of pretty woman Julia Roberts and
crooner Lyle Lovett in 1993 made many a
jaw drop. After all, what could they possibly
have in common? Apparently, not much. By
1995, the Oscar winner and the singer called
it quits after it was alleged that they barely
spent any time together. Pretty weird, eh?

Bumper Snickers!

HONK IF YOU SLEPT WITH CLINTON!
Monica Lewinsky

ALL MEN ARE IDIOTS, AND I MARRIED THEIR KING.
Camilla Parker Bowles

Say It Ain't So!

Products or organizations that celebs should never endorse:

Dan Quayle for Hooked on Phonics

Lindsay Lohan for Smirnoff

Bernard Goetz for Subway

Mary-Kate Olsen for Hometown Buffet

Stupid Says . . .

❝It's really hard to maintain a one-on-one relationship if the other person is not going to allow me to be with other people.**❞**
—Axl Rose, lead singer of Guns N' Roses

Just Say Duh!

Once upon a time there were two little Mouseketeers. One was a little blonde tart who wore underwear. The other was a squeaky voiced imp who didn't yet have a sexy back. When they sorta grew up, they became the king and queen of Popdom, cute as two mice in a hayfield. Theirs was a love that represented all things sweet and terminally virginal. Then, one horrible day, the pubescent duo walked through the doors of Splitsville. The little tart continued to maintain her pure-as-snow demeanor, but her former mouse-ke-hunk turned rat, and let the cat out of the bag that Snow White was no longer a vestal virgin. The moral of the story? If you're gonna keep a secret—make sure it's in sync.

Leave a Message!

Simon Cowell:
For the love of all things human . . . you call that a message? I don't answer to someone whose voice sounds like a constipated moose and whose hair looks like Liberace with his finger in a light socket. You can reach Sanjaya at 1.800.SUCKUP.

Wedded Miss

Zsa Zsa Gabor is among an elite group of serial marriers, but her eighth wedding in particular crossed the absurd line. On April 13, 1982, the feisty Hungarian wed Mexican actor Felipe de Alba. On April 14, the marriage, which apparently took place on a ship, was annulled given that Gabor wasn't legally divorced from hubby number seven. Gabor has had a total of nine better halves, including Burhan Belge, Conrad Hilton, George Sanders, Hurbert Hutner, Joshua S. Cosden, Jack Ryan, Michael O'Hara, Alba, and the now infamous Anna Nicole Smith lover/paternity seeker Prince Frederic von Anhalt. And before you ask: Yes, Gabor is related by marriage to Paris Hilton. Let it sink in. . . .

Don't Quote Me

Match the lamebrained quote to the celeb who uttered it:

Brad Pitt
Jennifer Lopez
Elton John

Jean-Claude Van
Damme
Pamela Anderson

1. There is nothing wrong with going to bed with someone of your own sex. People should be very free with sex, they should draw the line at goats.
2. I'm one of those people you hate because of genetics. It's the truth.
3. I've been fortunate—I haven't had too many auditions. I slept with the right people.
4. I admit I do have a very nice butt. Some say my career was built on it!
5. I judge people on how they smell, not how they look.

Answers:
1-Elton John.
2-Brad Pitt.
3-Pamela Anderson.
4-Jean-Claude Van
Damme.
5-Jennifer Lopez.

Clueless Wonders

Questions that simpleminded celebs don't understand:

Question: Have you ever been to Winn-Dixie?

Answer: I don't like country music festivals.

Unholy Matrimony

E.T., the Extra-Terrestrial, has another connection to *Forbes* celeb divorce list, this time ranking fourth. The film's screenwriter, Melissa Mathison married Harrison Ford in 1983. By 2001, the marriage went kaput and Indiana Jones began dating *Ally McBeal* waif Calista Flockhart. By 2004, Mathison and Ford sealed the deal to the tune of $85 million, with Mathison even getting a percentage of the former Han Solo's future income for any revenue generated from films he made while they were hitched. Ain't love grand?

Diva Darlings—Not!

Everyone makes bad career choices, but when celebs make bad decisions we're all there to watch the trainwreck. Unfortunately, for most of these daft buggers, they have the audacity to quit television shows when they're at the top of their game, thinking they'll easily become big screen stars. In 1976, Farrah Fawcett signed on for the jiggle television that was *Charlie's Angels*. A year later, she flew the coop for bigger and better things. Bad move. While she did earn award nods for *The Burning Bed* and *Extremities*, dreams of A-list accolades were as elusive as Charlie. A similar fate befell David Caruso whose big breakthrough arrived in the form of *NYPD Blue* in 1993. After major accolades and award nominations, Caruso bailed just after the second season started. He went on to make the major flop *Jade* and the ironically named *Kiss of Death*. Of course, Caruso managed a major comeback in 2002 on *CSI Miami,* but others rarely have that luck. Just ask Shelley Long and the cast of *Seinfeld*.

What's in a Name?

Have you noticed over the past few years that the media has become weirdly obsessed with mangling the names of celebrity couples? A-list couples change as often as a newborn's Pampers, and as if they didn't have enough trouble maintaining some semblance of a normal relationship, do they really need a stupid nickname? And why is the guy's name usually first? We've got Brangelina, TomKat, Bennifer, Vaughniston, Spederline, and some of the more bizarre incarnations like Garfleck (Jennifer Garner and Ben Affleck) and Ashmi (Ashton Kutcher and Demi Moore). In the past, there were no schmancy nics for A-listers, so it's likely that we've got Bennifer to blame for all the nonsense, since it appears they started the whole brouhaha. Let's all just bow our heads and give thanks that Biggie Smalls and Dick Clark never hooked up.

Favorite Movies of the Truly Daft

Posh Spice:
Spend it Like Beckham

William Shatner:
Finding Nimoy

O.J. Simpson:
An Affair to Dismember

Martha Stewart:
Romeo is Weeding

Stupid Says . . .

"If you have intercourse you run the risk of dying and the ramifications of death are final.**"**

—Cyndi Lauper

Bosom Buddies

Super Bowl 2004 is an event that everyone will remember—but not for the athletics. Approximately 140 million viewers were tuned in to the main event, which boasted a half-time show featuring Justin Timberlake and Janet Jackson. Unfortunately, everyone saw more of Jackson than needed. At the end of the song "Rock Your Body," Timberlake pulled at Jackson's corset while warbling, "gonna have you naked by the end of this song."

No truer words were ever spoken.

In a split second, out popped Jackson's right hooter. Mothers covered their children's eyes, politicians got on their moral soapboxes, and the FCC blew its stack quicker than you could say Vesuvius. Some call it a wardrobe malfunction, others remain unconvinced that Jackson's actions were completely innocent. In the end, nobody won. Not show producers MTV, not Jackson, not the networks, and certainly not the general public who has since been reintroduced to the word *censorship*. It was the breast seen 'round the world, and we're still paying dearly for a glimpse of it. Thanks for the mammary, Janet.

Nitwit Neuroses

Diddycombaphobia:
Fear of indecisiveness

Keanuphobia:
Fear of Idaho

Anistonophobia:
Fear of breakups

Doleaphobia:
Fear of Viagra

Oh Baby!

Some of the names celebs bestow upon their progeny would never occur to us mere mortals. For example, Christie Brinkley's daughter Sailor Lee, Sonny and Cher's daughter Chastity, or John Travolta and Kelly Preston's son Jett. But what is one to do with former INXS lead singer Michael Hutchence whose daughter was dubbed Heavenly Hiraani Tiger Lily? What do you call her for short? Heavy Tiger?

Jailbirds

Oscar nominated thespian Robert Downey Jr.'s brilliant acting talents and impressive film career have long been overshadowed by his struggles with alcohol and drug addiction. In 1996, Downey was pulled over for speeding and arrested when heroin and an unloaded pistol were found in his vehicle. Given a three-year suspended prison sentence, Downey embarked on a seemingly determined path to "unsuspending" his sentence. After three subsequent arrests that involved sentencing to rehab clinics, a California judge finally invoked the three-year prison stint; as the judge put it, "To save your life." On the heels of an early release from the big house, Downey was twice more arrested in 2000 and 2001, and got himself booted off the cast of *Ally McBeal* in the process. More court ordered trips to rehab may have finally helped Downey stay clean and sober, but we're not holding our breath.

Nitwit Neuroses

Deppaphobia:
Fear of reversible tattoos

Farrahphobia:
Fear of coherent speech

Lewinskaphobia:
Fear of Gap dresses

Clintophobia:
Fear of Cuban stogies

Unholy Matrimony

Divorce was no field of dreams for *Robin Hood* star Kevin Costner and his wife Cindy Silva. Married in 1978, they split sixteen years later. According to *Forbes*, their disunion ranks sixth on the settlement scale, with Silva raking in a cool $80 million. No doubt, Costner might have recouped that had *Waterworld* actually generated more than forty dollars in ticket sales.

Say It Ain't So!

Products or organizations that celebs should never endorse:

Michael Jackson for Pampers

Pamela Anderson for WonderBra

Mel Gibson for Old Milwaukee

Pee Wee Herman for Orville Redenbacher

Oh Baby!

Sometimes ya just gotta shake your head and wonder. Nicholas Cage has always been a bit baffling in general and that is perhaps no more apparent than when he named his son Kal-el—Superman's birth name. Then there's Korn singer Jonathan Davis and his porn star wife Devin Davis who named their son Pirate. And if that doesn't make your head spin, try rationalizing the name Jason Lee gave his son: Pilot Inspektor. You can't make this stuff up.

On the Web

Shannen Doherty
www.unluckycharm.com

Martha Stewart
www.feloniouscooks.com

George W. Bush
www.icantpronouncenuclear.com

Paris Hilton
www.iamuseless.com

Body Art Gone Bad

Having a tattoo is a major decision for anyone, especially for a celeb whose body is under constant scrutiny. A few inked celebs learned the hard way that having their better half's name tattooed on a body part can be a major faux pas. After his breakup with Winona Ryder, Johnny Depp changed his ink from "Winona Forever," to "Wino Forever." Pamela Anderson altered her "Tommy" assignation to read "Mommy," and "Billy Bob" is no longer adorning the svelte arm of Angelina Jolie. Good thing Liz Taylor and Zsa Zsa didn't take up the practice.

Skeletons in the Closet

While most people are amused by celebrity mugshots for minor offensives (think Ryan O'Neal, Nick Nolte, and Mel Gibson), there are several celebrities whose close family members have committed murder. In 1979, Woody Harrelson's father Charles was convicted of killing a U.S. district judge just outside the judge's home. The prosecution claimed that a notorious drug dealer had hired Harrelson to kill the judge because he was known for handing out harsh sentences. Harrelson received two life sentences and died in prison in March 2007.

Future Oscar winner Charlize Theron was just a teenager when she saw her mother Gerda shoot and kill her husband and Charlize's natural father in self defense. Charles Theron was reportedly an abusive alcoholic and had attacked Gerda in a drunken rage. No charges were ever filed. In 1958, the late Lana Turner was in the midst of a tumultuous relationship with a gangster named Johnny Stompanato. During a particularly violent argument, Turner's teenage daughter Cheryl Crane stabbed Stompanato to death in fear for her mother's life. The killing was later deemed justifiable homicide.

Mix and Mingle:
Annoying Celeb Anagrams

Jude Law

Naomi Campbell

Kate Moss

George Michael

Michael Jackson

Howard Stern

Monica Lewinsky

Charlie Sheen

Madonna

Roseanne Barr

1. CANINE MILKYSOW
2. LEACH HENSIRE
3. MACHS ALIENJOCK
4. HARDEN WORTS
5. RERAN EARSNOB
6. JAW DUEL
7. GRIMACE EELHOG
8. A MANNOD
9. MAMBA CONEPILL
10. MAKE SOTS

Answers:
1-Monica Lewinsky.
2-Charlie Sheen.
3-Michael Jackson.
4-Howard Stern.
5-Roseanne Barr.
6-Jude Law.
7-George Michael.
8-Madonna.
9-Naomi Campbell.
10-Kate Moss.

The Mother of All Foot in Mouth Awards

Michael Richards, best known for his role as Kramer on the *Seinfeld* sitcom, suffered an on-stage meltdown in 2006 at the Laugh Factory comedy club in West Hollywood, California that hoisted him straight into national news. Responding to heckling from African American patrons of the club, Richards launched into a frenzy of racial slurs and epithets that lasted for nearly three minutes. The videotaped episode quickly made its way onto the Internet, which effectively squelched Richard's initial dismissals of the report as being blown out of proportion. According to professional comics and publicists who specialize in media spin, Michael Richards' budding stand-up comedy career was effectively ruined by his unforgivable performance. Word has it that even *Seinfeld's* infamous "soup Nazi" is boiling mad.

Deep Thoughts

If Pee Wee Herman invented a new portopotty, would it be called a Wee Wee Herman?

Bumper Snickers!

LIFE'S A BEACH, AND THEN YOU DROWN.
David Hasselhoff

I LIKE YOU BUT I WOULDN'T WANT
TO SEE YOU WORKING WITH
SUB-ATOMIC PARTICLES.
Steven Hawkings

Leave a Message!

Jessica Simpson:
*Hey Y'all! I'm real darn sorry I missed your
. . . oh wait. Is this thing on? How does this
work? Am I supposed to hit the button now?
What's the red light? Dayum.*

He Said, She Said

Question: What's the best way to kill a relationship?

Answer: Sleep with your children's nanny and then make a public apology to your beloved fiancée via the press verifying that you are guilty as charged.

The relationship of Jude Law and Sienna Miller was moving along wonderfully with an announcement of an engagement in 2004. In 2005 however, Daisy Wright, the nanny to Law's three children from his marriage to actress Sadie Frost, gave an interview to a British newspaper providing juicy details of her sex life with Law. She reported Law to be, "a masterful lover who made my whole body tingle." Miller broke off the engagement, but they continued to have an on again, off again relationship until late 2006 when they finally called it quits. The rest of the world in the meantime wondered what took her so long?

WHY IS MR. POTATO HEAD
JEALOUS
OF MICHAEL JACKSON?

M I C H A E L
JACKSON
HAS HAD MORE NOSES

Love Is a Many Splendored Bling

We've seen some unearthly couplings, but perhaps none caused as much media frenzy as Jennifer Lopez and Ben Affleck. The claim by J. Lo that, "we're just normal people" combined with the blatant overindulgences (the six carat pink diamond ring, his-and-her Bentleys, etc.), and Affleck's alleged gambling and strip club panderings made this odd couple look like a pair of ventriloquist dummies. When the big bust-up finally occurred, days before their wedding, who wasn't relieved? Affleck himself said it best when he described how he felt after the relationship was over:

It's the sort of vague calm you get after vomiting, where the vomit itself is rather unpleasant but when it's over it does bring you a kind of strange peace, and that's how I feel.

"Bennifer" actually had the gall to blame their split on the media, who did go a bit nuts from 2002 to 2004, but the odd couple gave them plenty of tabloid hash. Both have moved on and married other celebs, but their lavish and very public lifestyle of the rich and famous was a horrendous trainwreck of celebrity absurdity. Oh . . . and they'll never *ever* be forgiven for *Jersey Girl* or *Gigli*. 'Nuff said.

Gee Whiz

"Gee whiz" was indeed the apparently unofficial reaction of Prince Ernst August, the husband of Monaco's Princess Caroline, as he toured the 2000 World's Fair in Hanover, Germany. Near the Turkish Pavilion, the Prince was overcome by the urge to relieve himself, and did so—right out in the open. The blue-blooded whizzer and his spin doctors vehemently denied allegations of the royal dousing, until a snapshot taken by an alert schoolgirl surfaced in a German tabloid. Faced with indisputable proof, Ernst took out a full-page ad in another German newspaper and apologized for the act, while denying that he actually violated the Turkish Pavilion itself or the Turkish people indirectly. The Prince and Princess seemed hopeful that the public backsplash would soon peter out.

Favorite Movies of the Truly Daft

Laura Bush: Conan the Librarian

Tatum O'Neal: Gone with the Windbag

Simon Cowell: Jurassic Snark

Prince Charles: Two Weddings and a Funeral

Nitwit Neuroses

Judeaphobia:
Fear of nannies

Noltephobia:
Fear of sanity

Electraphobia:
Fear of Dennis Rodman

Diva Darlings—Not!

There are few celebs who actually find success when they have a talk show. Think Oprah, Donahue, Carson, Springer, Rosie, Ellen, Larry King, and Letterman. Unfortunately, a host of celebs felt they had the charm and charisma to hold their own. Boy were they deluded. Arsenio Hall, Ricki Lake, and Dennis Miller gave it a good run, but others weren't so lucky. Memorable celebs who bombed include Magic Johnson, Chevy Chase, Tom Green, Tony Danza, Megan Mullally, Morton Downey Jr., Carnie Wilson, Richard Simmons, Gabrielle Carteris, and Sharon Osbourne. Johnson's show barely lasted two months, and John McEnroe's primetime show had such deplorable ratings that they didn't even register on the Nielsen Ratings meter.

Wedded Miss

Ace Ventura maniac Jim Carrey musta flipped his lid when he married former *Picket Fences* cutie Lauren Holly. Married in 1996, the tumultuous pair, who had a history of breaking up, lasted a mere nine months. Infamous ear nipper Mike Tyson and former *Head of the Class* star Robin Givens didn't fare any better in 1988. Much to nobody's surprise, Givens accused Tyson of spousal abuse and they divorced in 1989. Givens didn't have much luck in 1997 either. On August 22, she married Syetozar Marinkovic. On August 22, she also divorced him!

Stupid Says . . .

❝If you could live forever, would you and why?❞

❝I would not live forever, because we should not live forever, because if we were supposed to live forever, then we would live forever, but we cannot live forever, which is why I would not live forever.❞

—Miss Alabama at the 1994 Miss USA Pageant

Candy is Dandy

If scatterbrained celebs had candy bars named after them, what would they be?

Tom Cruise: Mission Uncrunchable

Alec Baldwin: Baby Ruthless

Madonna: S&Ms

Britney Spears: Three Mouseketeers

Tom Sizemore: Smackers

Keith Richards: Tweaks

Anna Nicole Smith: Sugar Daddy's

Kevin Federline: Mrs. Goodbar

Sean Penn: Nestle's Punch

Katie Holmes: KidKat

Bill Gates: Bit-O-Money

Oprah Winfrey: Pounds

Paris Hilton: 100 Billion Dollar
Grandiose Bar

Clueless Wonders

Questions that simpleminded celebs don't understand:

Question: Would you like some M&Ms?

Answer: I'm not into bondage.

Just Say Duh!

Bill Gates, founder of Microsoft and one of the richest men on the planet, has had a few run-ins with the law, all of which occurred behind the wheel. In 1977, Gates was pulled over in Albuquerque, New Mexico for speeding. The police report for the incident has mysteriously vanished from Albuquerque police records, but the speed Mr. Gates was traveling at was apparently impressive enough to get him arrested and hauled to the slammer. The only remaining records of the incident are mugshots of the smiling twenty-one-year-old über-geek. When the photographs surfaced and began circulating on the Internet, it was none other than Gates himself who filled in missing details about the incident. Records that vanish? Sounds like Windows XP.

Apocalyptic Stupidity

A hot Aussie lad named Mel
Was drinking one night for a spell
Then the cops called him out
Like a rogue he did shout
And then his career went to hell!

Jailbirds

In 1961 Al Pacino was only twenty-one-years-old and a struggling young actor when a car he was riding in with two companions was pulled over by police in Providence, Rhode Island. A .38-caliber handgun was found in the trunk, and the three young men were arrested and hauled to the pokey for carrying a concealed weapon. Pacino reportedly explained that he and his companions were actors on their way to a skit and that the pistol was merely a prop. It seems that Pacino, who was broke at the time, couldn't make bail and wound up spending three days behind bars before being released. By all accounts, Pacino's explanation was a convincing enough performance for the local prosecutor to decline pursuing charges. Think he knew he was messing with Scarface?

Deep Thoughts

If Al Gore became a bullfighter, would he be
called Al Gored?

Favorite Movies of the Truly Daft

Jennifer Lopez: Lord of the Blings:
Return of the Ring

Ellen DeGeneres: A Few Good Women

Dick Cheney: Willy Wonky and the
Chemical Factory

Monica Lewinsky: Dressed to Spill

Stupid Says . . .

❝He speaks English, Spanish, and he's
bilingual too.**❞**

—Don King

Pimp My Ride

Isaiah Washington:
Chevy Impalogize

Pamela Anderson:
Subaru Busty

Ringo Starr:
Dodge Duringo

William Shatner:
Chevy Phaser

Nitwit Neuroses

Trumpaphobia:
Fear of combovers

Hasslehoffaphobia:
Fear of *Baywatch*

Pamaphobia:
Fear of silicone

Croweaphobia:
Fear of long distance carriers

Royal Blunders

In an incident outside a London nightclub in 2004, England's Prince Harry responded to a pushy gaggle of paparazzi by shoving a camera into the face of the photographer who had the ill fortune of being closest to his Royal Surliness. The photographer suffered a minor cut to his lip, along with a major blow to his ego. The Royal Prosecutor declined to look into the matter.

In 2007, the littlest prince had improved his nightclub departure strategy by cleverly slipping out the back door of another social hot spot in the wee hours of the morning, only to stroll straight into the lenses of equally clever photographers. Uttering an unprincely epithet, Harry lunged at the photographers and had to be restrained—and then manhandled—toward his waiting limo by a level-headed bodyguard. The photographers who weren't running for their lives got their revenge by snapping shots of the prince as he drunkenly miscalculated the step into the limousine and fell flat on his royal derriere.

They Said *What?*

Fred and Ethel Mertz, the cranky fun-loving friends and landlords of Lucy and Ricky Ricardo had great on-screen chemistry, so few would guess that they despised each other in real life. William Frawley and Vivian Vance had a long-running feud which continued until Frawley died in 1966. Vance didn't care for his cantankerous personality, and was insulted that a much older man was playing her husband (there was over twenty-years difference between them and she felt that he should be playing her father). In turn, Frawley found her attitude offensive. When *I Love Lucy* ended, the duo were offered a spin-off series of their own. Frawley was willing to go for it despite their animosity, because of the financial gain. Vance however, nixed the idea because she had no interest in continuing a working relationship with him. He never forgave her for this, and Vance continued her loathing of him. Vance, in fact, was dining in a restaurant with her husband when she heard of Frawley's death. Her reaction? She reportedly shouted, "champagne for everyone!"

Unholy Matrimony

Ranked number six on *Forbes* celeb divorce meter is legendary Beatle Sir Paul McCartney and his second wife, charity campaigner Heather Mills. It should come as no surprise to anyone that marrying a Beatle can be a nasty sordid pubic nightmare. Just ask Yoko Ono. For Macca, as Sir Paul was dubbed by the British press, and Lady Macca that nightmare was worse than anything Freddy Krueger could dream up. In 2006, after four years of marriage, they announced their divorce. From there, negotiations sunk faster than a yellow submarine. After a long and winding road to court, the matter was finally settled. Mills is said to have received $144 million of her former husband's estimated $700 million fortune. All you need is love and a damn good lawyer, eh?

Say It Ain't So!

Products or organizations that celebs should never endorse:

Mariah Carey for the Christian Children's Fund

Dick Cheney for *Guns and Ammo*

Bill Gates for Andersen Windows

Kevin Federline for DHL

On the Web

Dan Quayle
www.yousaytomatoe.com

Bill Gates
www.windowsxpwontboot.com

Lindsay Lohan
www.iamnotafirecrotch.com

Isaiah Washington
www.ikilledmycareer.com

Monikers of the Self-Important

Isn't it fascinating that some celebs are so damned important that their nickname alone is enough to identify them? How are we supposed to deal with that? Are we required to bow to "The Donald" or "The Governator"? Curtsy to the "King of Pop" or alternately be frightened of "Wacko Jacko"? Be in awe of "The Italian Stallion" or "The Rock"? Or just sit around and quilt with "The Material Girl" or "Jenny on the Block"? Guess we should all be thankful that Bill Clinton was nicknamed "Bubba" and not "The Cigar."

WHY DID BILL CLINTON
STOP PLAYING THE
SAXOPHONE?

HE WAS TOO BUSY
PLAYING
THE HORMONICA

Just Say Duh!

Denise Richards, the actress, former Playboy Playmate, and ex-wife of Charlie Sheen, had a bit of a hissy one night. Imagine that. It appears that during a photo shoot while filming a movie with Pamela Anderson, Richards snatched a laptop computer from the hands of an annoying photographer, and hucked it over the side of a balcony at the River Rock Hotel and Casino in Richmond, British Columbia. News reports originally claimed that the laptop struck and injured a wheelchair-bound pensioner on the floor below, which temporarily raised the outrage ante on blondie's 2006 outburst.

As the truth unfolded, however, the only injury inflicted was to the laptop itself, which was terminal. The Royal Mounted Police investigated but decided the issue was a civil matter and declined to pursue criminal charges. Richards apologized for the incident and agreed to pay for damages. It's a crying shame that the laptop couldn't afford to hire Debra Opri.

Leave a Message!

Paris Hilton:
Hi. This is Paris. If you're worth more than ten million, press one. If you own a Gulf Stream, press two. If you're trying to reach me in prison, press three. If your daddy's a billionaire, press the pound sign to page me.

The Honorary NRA
Idiotic Argument Award

As a result of a 1996 mass shooting in Dunblane, Scotland, the British population demanded tougher firearms restrictions in a nation already know for strict gun control. Within weeks, more than 22,000 unwanted or illegal firearms were voluntarily handed over to authorities. In counterpoint, Prince Philip, the often outrageously outspoken husband of Queen Elizabeth, made this absurdly disturbing observation: "If a cricketer, for instance, suddenly decided to go into a school and batter a lot of people to death with a cricket bat, which he could do very easily, I mean, are you going to ban cricket bats?"

Blooming Idiots

Match the celeb with their favorite flower:

a. Callous Lily
b. Sweet Pee
c. Status
d. Snotdragon
e. Gladiators
f. Hyderangeia
g. Twolips
h. Larkspurned
i. Ninny of the Valley
j. Criesatmymum

1. Jessica Simpson
2. Anna Nicole Smith
3. Russell Crowe
4. Pee Wee Herman
5. Mick Jagger
6. Mel Gibson
7. Alec Baldwin
8. Sean Young
9. Paris Hilton
10. Donald Trump

Answers: 1-i,
2-j, 3-e, 4-b,
5-g, 6-a, 7-h,
8-f, 9-d, 10-c

Stupid Says . . .

❝I loved Jordan. He was one of the greatest athletes of our time.**❞**
    —Mariah Carey after learning of the death of King Hussein of Jordan

Oh Baby!

Sometimes celebs have a theme when naming their offspring. *Spy Kids* director Robert Rodriguez and his wife Elizabeth Avellan have a thing for "R" names. Daughter Rhiannon's name is simple enough, but they got creative when it came to naming their sons: Rocket Valentin, Racer Maximilliano, Rebel Antonio, and Rogue. Forrest Whitaker took a more Zen approach, naming his son Ocean, and his daughters Autumn, Sonnet, and True.

Foot in Mouth Award

Faux Brit Gwyneth Paltrow found herself neck-deep in the Thames in December 2006 when she gave an interview to a Portuguese publication. In the interview, she commented that she liked living in the United Kingdom because "I don't fit into the bad side of American psychology. The British are much more intelligent and civilized than the Americans." She went on to say that she loved the English lifestyle because "It's not as capitalistic as America. People don't talk about work and money, they talk about interesting things at dinner." Of course, Shakespeare's dream girl later whined to *People* magazine that she was severely misquoted. Tsk tsk. Bear in mind that little Miss Haughty was voted "Most Stuck Up" in the October 1998 *Movieline's* 100 Most issue. Oh dear. And there's that wee little matter of her stating, "I would rather die than let my kid eat Cup-A-Soup."

All this coming from the gal who donned a 200-pound fat suit to star in *Shallow Hal*. Go figure.

Diva Darlings—Not!

When mortal couples have a child they're always eager to show photographs to anyone willing to take a peek. This wasn't the case for Tom Cruise. Not long after he launched his attack on Oprah's couch, it was announced that he and Cruise incubator Katie Holmes were expecting. Of course the announcement generated more frenzy than an asteroid due to hit earth the day after tomorrow. For nine months, the world ticked off the days until this new messiah took her first breath. And what did everyone get for their trouble? Nothing. Zip. Not a single glimpse of the TomKat spawn since her April 2006 birthdate. Baby Suri Cruise was an enigma, and the flash soon hit the tabloid fire: She must have been adopted, or deformed, was an alien baby, or simply didn't exist at all. Brangelina did the right thing and immediately unleashed pics of genetically perfect Shiloh Nouvelle after she was born—and they gave the photo profits to charity. But like her daddy, Suri Cruise was Mission Impossible. It wasn't until October that the wee Cruise missile was publicly revealed in *Vanity Fair* magazine. It would appear that the speculation of whether or not she's of alien origin is still in question.

HOW DOES GEORGE W.

BUSH

GO THROUGH THE

FOREST?

HE TAKES THE

PSYCHO
PATH

He Said, She Said

Gary Coleman, the diminutive star of
Diff'rent Strokes fell on tough times after
the show was canceled in 1986 after an
eight-year run. Two years after the show
ended, Coleman wound up suing his parents
for misappropriating the nearly $18 million
he'd made on the sitcom, and ultimately
received close to $4 million in a settlement.
That same year, Coleman was involved in an
altercation with a fan, Tracy Fields, after
she asked for his autograph. Accounts of the
incident vary, but Coleman was arrested for
assault after reportedly punching the
woman several times. He eventually pleaded
guilty to a charge of disturbing the peace
and received a one-year suspended sentence
and a year of anger management classes. The
pint-size puncher avoided a formal civil suit
brought against him by Fields by airing the
case with her on *People's Court,* a reality-
based court program. The appearance was
probably not the television comeback Coleman was hoping for. In the end, he was
ordered to pay $1,650 in hospital bills for
Fields' injuries, but the woman's request for
additional cash for pain and suffering was
denied. Next time he probably shouldn't pick
on a woman who's twice his size.

Bumper Snickers!

VERY FUNNY, SCOTTY.
NOW BEAM DOWN MY CLOTHES.
William Shatner

YOUR LUCKY NUMBERS ARE 4, 8, 15, 16,
23, 42. WATCH FOR THEM EVERYWHERE.
Jorge Garcia of Lost

Nitwit Neuroses

Marykateophobia:
Fear of buffets

Billybobophobia:
Fear of blood banks

Evanderholyphobia:
Fear of Mike Tyson

Joanaphobia:
Fear of facelifts

They Said *What?*

In 1983, Paul McCartney and Michael Jackson got together for the duet "Say, Say, Say," a seemingly harmless show of musicality that as it turned out, was the precursor to a clash of the titans. In hindsight, McCartney made the mistake of mentioning to Jacko that there was money to be made in purchasing rights to songs. What did the nosy one do? He outbid McCartney in 1984 when the former Beatle attempted to buy back the rights to the Beatles songs. During the 1990s, Yoko Ono stepped up to the plate when McCartney wanted some of the writing credits on several of the Beatles hits to show his name first and not John Lennon's. After much feuding, the credits remained unaltered.

Stupid Says . . .

I performed at Mom and Dad's party when I was four. Oh my gosh, I was singing a Madonna song and I peed myself.**

—Britney Spears

Unholy Matrimony

The *Titanic* wasn't the only thing that was sunk when it came to director James Cameron's divorce to his fourth wife, *Terminator* tough-gal Linda Hamilton. What appeared to be a rather tumultuous two-year marriage, from 1997 to 1999, ended with Hamilton walking off with an estimated settlement of over $50 million. That chunk of plunder landed this divorce at number seven on *Forbes* list. For his part, an undaunted Cameron married *Titanic* actress Suzy Amis in 2000. One can only hope that Cameron's mantra for divorce court isn't "I'll be back."

On the Web

Tori Spelling
www.poorlittlerichgirl.org

Charlie Sheen
www.howmuchdoyoucharge.com

George Michael
www.passthedoobie.com

Prince Charles
www.questionablegeneaology.org

HOW MANY BALDWIN BROTHERS
DOES IT TAKE TO SCREW IN
A LIGHT BULB?

ONLY ONE—BILLY. DANIEL IS
BUSY STEALING CARS AND
ATTENDING REHAB.
STEPHEN IS BUSY BEING
A TRAVELING PREACHER.
AND ALEC IS BUSY TRYING
TO GRASP THE CONCEPT OF
**A N G E R
MANAGEMENT**

Pimp My Ride

Tim Allen: Hyundai Santa Fake

Pee Wee Herman: Chevy Excitation

David Hasselhoff: Lamborweinie

Gwyneth Paltrow: VW Smug

Accidents Happen

Michael Hutchence, front man and general hellraiser for the band INXS, brought the band's anagramatic name into stark reality at the Ritz-Carlton Hotel in Sydney, Australia in 1997. Hutchence was found hanging in his hotel room and was thought to have committed suicide until his long-time girlfriend, Paula Yates shed some disconcerting light on the incident. Yates insisted that Hutchence was far from suicidal, and had in fact just been trying to have a little fun when he accidentally killed himself while practicing auto-erotic asphyxiation. It appears that Hutchence was in the habit of choking himself to near unconsciousness in order to heighten sexual self-pleasure. The death was ultimately ruled accidental, but his lack of common sense was most definitely in excess.

Royal Blunders

Princess Michael of Kent, the former Baroness Marie-Christine Agnes Hedwig Ida von Reibnitz, made international headlines in 2004 by angrily suggesting to a boisterous group of African American diners at a posh restaurant in New York that, "You guys should go back to the colonies."

The Princess simultaneously denied and defended her intemperate remarks, saying that she had been misrepresented, and that anyway, the diners to whom she did not make the comment were just "a group of rappers." For the record, the diners were a media executive, an investment banker, a television reporter, an entertainment lawyer, and a fashion correspondent. According to one member of the party, the Princess' behavior left the high profile patrons "stupefied."

Favorite Movies of the Truly Daft

Dick Cheney: Raging Bullcrap

Karl Malden: The Wizard of Schnozz

Anne Heche: Nightmare on Realm Street

Justin Timberlake: Pirates of the Caribbean: Dead Man's Breast

Don't Quote Me

Match the lamebrained quote to the celeb who uttered it:

Christina Aguilera   David Hasselhoff
Keanu Reeves   Michael Jackson
Courtney Love

1. The most loving thing to do is to share your bed with someone.
2. So, where's the Cannes Film Festival being held this year?
3. I've got taste. It's inbred in me.
4. I cried over beauty, I cried over pain, and the other time I cried because I felt nothing. I can't help it. I'm just a cliche of myself.
5. I used to do drugs, but don't tell anyone or it will ruin my image.

Answers:
1-Michael Jackson.
2-Christina Aguilera.
3-David Hasselhoff.
4-Keanu Reeves.
5-Courtney Love.

Here Kitty Kitty . . .

Most people think that A-list actresses are simply chosen for a part and never have to audition. Unfortunately, even the highest paid actresses have to prove they're right for a part. In 1992, the role of Catwoman in Tim Burton's film *Batman Returns* was a hot commodity. Burton originally cast Annette Bening, but she had to pull out upon becoming pregnant, so the coveted role went to Michelle Pfeiffer. That choice didn't sit well with Sean Young, who was hired to play Vicki Vale in the original *Batman,* but after an on-set accident gave up the part to Kim Basinger. To prove her point, Young showed up on the *Batman Returns* set wearing full Catwoman regalia and confronted Burton about his poor casting. Unsuccessful in her attempts she then went public with her campaign, appearing on *The Joan Rivers Show* in her cat suit, and continued disparaging Burton. Needless to say, Young's incessant meowing sent her and her career straight to the pound.

Jailbirds

Former *Home Alone* cutie Macaulay Culkin spent less than an hour in the Oklahoma City Jail before posting bond for an illegal drug possession charge in 2004. Culkin was the only passenger in a rented vehicle driven by his friend and fellow actor Brett Tabisel when they were pulled over by City Police for speeding and illegal lane changes. When the officer asked Tabisel, who was a Tony Award nominee for Best Actor in a Musical in 1996, if there were any drugs in the vehicle, he said, "Oh, no, no. You can check the vehicle if you like." The officer took him up on the offer and found a plastic baggie of marijuana and a cigarette case containing a half-dozen rolled joints.

If ever there was a time for the goofy "aagghhh!" face Culkin made in the first *Home Alone* movie—this was it. Culkin pleaded guilty to misdemeanor charges and received a one-year suspended sentence and a $950 slap on the wrist. Next time he oughta try driving alone.

The Name Game

If these celebs had gotten together!

Winona Ryder and Don Knotts = WiKnot?

Madonna and Simon Cowell = MadCow

Candice Bergen and Ice Cube = Iceberg

Barbara Walters, Matt Damon, and Bing
Crosby = BaDaBing

Wedded Miss

Some marriages just aren't meant to be.
Case in point, the quickie Vegas nuptials of
Baywatch alum Carmen Electra and NBA
hoopster and increasingly odd character
Dennis Rodman. Wed in 1998, the odd couple officially divorced five months later,
though it's alleged that their union was
actually annulled after a few days. Under
the heading of blast from the past, is *Easy
Rider* Dennis Hopper and Mamas and the
Papas songbird Michelle Phillips who in
1970 were hitched for a whopping eight days!

They Said *What?*

Every generation has it's own unique vernacular—something that helps identify a certain era and its pop culture and climate. On occasion, however, a new word or phrase is uttered that sends the class quotient plummeting to a new low, especially if it's said by the young, rich, and exceptionally stupid. In May of 2006, during a night out with Paris Hilton, celebudunce oil heir Brandon Davis unleashed a poisonous rant aimed at Hilton rival Lindsay Lohan. His incessant blather claimed that La Lohan lacked personal hygiene, and that "she's worth about seven million, which means she's poor. It's disgusting. She lives in a motel." But that wasn't the worst of it. Above all, he dubbed her "fire crotch." All this while "innocent" Miss Hilton stood by and laughed. Davis did publicly apologize, but unfortunately, it's now become part of human history—a history that future anthropologists will one day study and ponder why ice cubes have higher I.Q.s than trust fund babies.

Bumper Snickers!

IF YOU CAN READ THIS . . . I CAN SLAM ON MY BRAKES AND SUE YOU.
Alan Dershowitz

THE EARTH IS FULL—GO HOME.
Marilyn Manson

Nitwit Neuroses

Oprahphobia:
Fear of Jenny Craig

Britophobia:
Fear of wigs

Slyophobia:
Fear of *Rocky* sequels

Jlopezophobia:
Fear of large derrieres

WHAT'S ELLEN BARKIN'S FAVORITE POSITION?

FACING TIFFANY'S

Leave a Message!

Melanie Griffith:
Hi it's Melanie. I'd love to hear from you, so leave a message at the beep. If you're calling for Antonio and you're under thirty I'll rip your head off. Have a nice day!

Deep Thoughts

If Paris Hilton made cheese, would it be called Paris Stilton?

The Last Laugh

Sometimes, you just never know what's gonna come out of someone's mouth—especially when it's from one celeb to another. During a party, introductions were made between jazz singer George Melly and Rolling Stone Mick Jagger. Upon meeting the big-lipped wonder, Melly said that he didn't expect Jagger to have so many wrinkles. Jagger replied, "They're not wrinkles. They're laughter lines." Melly's response was anything but subtle: "Really? Surely nothing could be that funny." Can someone actually get away with saying that to a Rolling Stone?

Just Say Duh!

In the run-up to the gubernatorial election in California in 2003, former body builder-turned actor-turned politician Arnold Schwarzenegger was accused by a half-dozen women of sexual harassment and groping incidents. The "Governator-to-be" admitted to having "behaved badly" in his younger years and offered a general apology to every woman he had ever offended, there apparently being too many to single out.

One of Schwarzenegger's accusers was British television host Anna Richardson, who sued the hands-on budding politician over a breast groping incident that occurred before cameras just after her television talk show in London. The year was 2000, just three years before the election, and Arnie was busily pimping his film *The Sixth Day* when he decided to develop a firsthand opinion of Richardson's claim that her assets were 100 percent natural. Schwarznegger's spin doctors recounted a fairly tame version of the snafu, but photographs hit the Internet and presented an explicit eyeful of a less than subtle handful. Arnie's professional handlers wisely avoided public scrutiny and made the problem go away by settling out of court. *Hasta la vista*, baby.

On the Web

Madonna
www.iamgandhi.com

Russell Crowe
www.caniuseyourphone.com

Bill Clinton
www.internsofamerica.org

Hillary Clinton
www.imarriedanidiot.com

Unholy Matrimony

Wall Street trading dropped a few notches the day Michael Douglas and his wife of twenty-three years, Diandra, finalized their divorce. Married in 1977, theirs was a rather nasty affair that resulted in Diandra receiving an estimated $45 million when all was said and done in the year 2000. That amount of cash landed them eighth on *Forbes* celeb divorce list. In that same year, Douglas took the plunge again with Welsh ingenue Catherine Zeta-Jones, the *Zorro*-full actress who is twenty-five years his junior.

Stupid Says . . .

66Rarely is the question asked, is our children learning?99

—George W. Bush

Princess Dubya?

In 2004, Prince Harry began what appears to be a serious relationship with Chelsy Davy, who was nineteen-years-old at the time. Miss Davy, who is a native of South Africa and the daughter of a millionaire safari operator, is reported to have earned an affectionate nickname, "Dubya," from her princely beau because of her bird-brained commentary.

Chelsy has been attributed with asking such inane questions such as, "Are wooly mammoths really extinct?" and "Why don't buffalo eat deer when they get hungry?" It appears that Chelsy should make a charming contribution to the royal intellectual treasure chest.

Favorite Movies of the Truly Daft

Charlie Sheen: Saving My Privates

Anne Coulter: To Spill a Mocking Word

Don Imus: Hoop Screams

Alec Baldwin: They Shoot Divorcees,
Don't They?

Foot in Mouth Award

Everyone is entitled to their own opinion, but on occasion, a high-profile celeb decides to go nose-to-the-wall and become Yankee Doodle Duncy. Piratical heartthrob Johnny Depp got in a bit of muck in 2003 when he commented to German news magazine *Stern* that "America is dumb," and "a dumb puppy that has big teeth that can bite and hurt you." He went on to say that he'd like his children to "see America as a toy, a broken toy. Investigate it a little, check it out, get this feeling, and then get out." Ahoy mateys! Ol' Captain Jack really walked the plank on that one!

Diva Darlings—Not!

Media guru and domestic know-it-all Martha Stewart built an empire out of her extraordinary talents in business and the public's taste for having the finer things in life explained in snooty detail. But in 2002, an un-ladylike stock trading oversight put her in the headlines and behind bars for five months—and it wasn't a "good thing." The U.S. Securities and Exchange Commission accused Stewart of dumping stocks she owned in the faltering ImClone pharmaceutical company. The alleged insider trading scheme avoided a loss of about $45,000 dollars, which is the equivalent of pocket lint for the uber-rich domestic demon. Had little 'ol Martha fessed up to the error, she probably would have received nothing more than a well-deserved scolding. Ironically, she was acquitted of the illegal trading charge, but convicted of lying about the deal. To rub imported sea salt into the wound: If Martha had hung onto the stock she would've made a profit on her holdings with ImClone. Tsk tsk. Shouldn't have dipped your hand into the Italian cookie jar, Ms. Stewart.

The Prince Philip Cultural Awareness Quiz

Which of the following comments is inaccurately attributed to England's Prince Philip?

1. During a visit to Australia in 2002, Prince Philip met with a congregation of Aboriginal leaders at a cultural park. At the meeting, the Prince asked, "Do you still throw spears at each other?"

2. On a trip to Papua, New Guinea, Prince Philip made this enlightened comment to a British student: "So, you managed not to get eaten then?"

3. Prince Philip graciously accepted a gift from a native in Kenya with the question: "You are a woman, aren't you?"

4. Upon meeting the president of Kenya, who was wearing traditional native Muslim robes, the Prince said: "You look like you're ready for bed!"

5. At a 1986 World Wildlife Fund Meeting in Beijing, Prince Philip made the observation: "If it has four legs and is not a chair, has wings and is not an aeroplane, or swims and is not a submarine, the Cantonese will eat it."

Answer: *Sadly, every comment is a pearl of politically and socially incorrect wisdom from Prince Philip's apparently endless supply of daft observations.*

Jailbirds

Many a celeb has been busted over the decades for various drug related infractions, especially marijuana. Robert Mitchum, Oliver Stone, Bob Denver, and Whitney Houston are just the tip of the perennial iceberg. And of course, there are the Beatles. John Lennon, George Harrison, and Paul McCartney have all been busted. During the 1970s and 1980s, McCartney was fined or arrested several times, but it was in 1980 at the Tokyo International Airport that McCartney ran into big trouble when officials found two bags of wacky weed in his suitcase. As a result, the Wings frontman served ten days in a Japanese prison, after which he was deported.

On the Web

Arnold Schwarzenegger
www.thanksforthegrope.com

Simon Cowell
www.crymeariver.org

Naomi Campbell
www.touchmeanddie.com

Gwyneth Paltrow
www.englisharesmarter.org

Divine Intervention

Terminally debonair Brit Hugh Grant made international headlines when he was busted for soliciting sex from Sunset Boulevard hooker Divine Brown in Hollywood in 1995. As a result of his bust, the *Music and Lyrics* star was slapped with a $400 fine for his indiscretion and ordered to take part in an AIDS awareness program. To his credit, the suave actor handled the scandal with uncommon aplomb for a celeb literally caught with his pants down. He hit the talk show circuit with unusual candor, and the press and public completely fell for his charming show of contrition. The hooker Grant propositioned, however, managed to wrangle a short-term cottage industry out of her new found fame, appearing on television programs hosted by Howard Stern and Danny Bonaduce. She also managed to get popped again in 1996 for loitering and prostitution in Las Vegas. Still, after making a couple of X-rated DVDs and hustling the British tabloids for all they were worth, Brown managed to capitalize on her infamy and turn a $60 trick into a *Pretty Woman* goldmine.

Pimp My Ride

Ryan O'Neal:
Chevy Maliboob

Anna Nicole Smith:
Dodge Tacomatose

Snoop Dogg:
Buick Beagle

Paris Hilton:
VW Cabriolayme

Leave a Message!

Kirstie Alley:
Have you called Jenny yet?

Stupid Says . . .

66 I never get bored, because there's always different puzzles, I'm wearing different clothes, there's different contestants, there's different prizes. 99
—Vanna White

Wedded Miss

Sometimes you've gotta wonder what celebs are thinking, don't you? On July 12, 1998, producer Robert Evans married fourth wife Catherine Oxenberg, blueblood and actress of *Dynasty* fame. He was sixty-eight, she was thirty-seven and had never been wed, so they got hitched after a whopping four-day courtship. Nine days later, their marriage was annulled. Equally daft was the marriage that resulted from the 2000 reality show *Who Wants to Marry a Multi-Millionaire?* Rick Rockwell chose and married Darva Conger on national television, but after the honeymoon, and information surfacing about a restraining order his previous fiancée had obtained, the primetime match went straight into the ratings dumper.

Nitwit Neuroses

Osbournaphobia:
Fear of profanity

Courtneylovaphobia:
Fear of drug testing

Gestophobia:
Fear of cabarets

Brandophobia:
Fear of Jabba the Hutt

Punch Drunk

Mickey Rourke's acting career has garnered a lot of attention for both his indisputable talent, and for his reputation as one of the most annoying and temperamental actors in cinematic history. Case in point, Alan Parker, director of *Angel Heart,* stated that, "working with Mickey is a nightmare." After a controversial sex scene with ex-Cosby kid Lisa Bonet in *Angel Heart,* and reports that Rourke had donated part of his acting salary to the terrorist group, the Irish Republican Army, Rourke's acting flame sputtered out. As all struggling actors do, Rourke turned to his alternate career choice, which in this case was professional boxing. In 1991, at the relatively geriatric age of thirty-eight, Rourke saw fair success in the ring against minor opponents, but he also suffered some major damage in his ill-conceived shot at success, getting his nose, ribs, and cheek broken, along with a split tongue and probably permanent brain damage. The experience may also have knocked some sense into Rourke. An intriguing facelift later, he has returned to minor acting roles on the big screen. Perhaps there's a part for him in *Rocky XXII*?

HOW MANY SUPERMODELS
DOES IT TAKE TO
SCREW IN A
LIGHT BULB?

JUST ONE. SHE SIMPLY
HOLDS IT IN PLACE AND
WAITS FOR THE
W O R L D
TO REVOLVE
AROUND HER.

Mix and Mingle:
Annoying Celeb Anagrams

Anna Nicole Smith	Heidi Fleiss
Snoop Dogg	Cameron Diaz
Sylvester Stallone	George Bush
Russell Crowe	Pee Wee Herman
Cindy Crawford	Kim Basinger

1. CELLUSERS ROW
2. RACY CROWDFIND
3. BIG RAMEKINS
4. BUGGER HOSE
5. ENEMA WHEEPER
6. INHALANT INCOMES
7. REALLY SVELTESNOTS
8. POND GOOS
9. DEFILE HISSI
10. ACID ARMZONE

Answers:
1-Russell Crowe.
2-Cindy Crawford.
3-Kim Basinger.
4-George Bush.
5-Pee Wee Herman.
6-Anna Nicole Smith.
7-Sylvester Stallone.
8-Snoop Dog.
9-Heidi Fleiss.
10-Cameron Diaz.

Favorite Movies of the Truly Daft

Jim Jones: Indiana Jones and
the Last Koolaid

Oprah Winfrey: Guess Who's Coming
to Slimfast?

George W. Bush: The Man Who Knew
Too Little

Gary Coleman: Legends of the Tall

Bumper Snickers!

WHERE THE HELL IS EASY STREET?
Heidi Fleiss

I SAID "NO" TO DRUGS, BUT THEY
JUST WOULDN'T LISTEN.
Robert Downey Jr.

Unholy Matrimony

Former Commodore Lionel Richie and his wife Diane Alexander made short work of their endless love in 2004 after a mere seven years of marriage. Richie is unfortunately no stranger to tabloid fodder of the day (any more than daughter Nicole currently is). Nicole's adoptive mother and Richie's first wife Brenda was actually arrested in 1988 for a host of infractions including vandalism, trespassing, and spousal abuse. Though they were already separated but not legally divorced (not until 1991), the chaos ensued when Brenda found Richie having a tête-a-tête with future wife Diane Alexander! Ranked ninth on *Forbes* celeb divorce list, it's estimated that Diane received around $20 million. Certainly that was enough to keep her dancing on the ceiling.

Say It Ain't So!

Products or organizations that celebs should never endorse:

Keith Richards for Diet Coke

Newt Gingrich for Geico

Julia Roberts for Nair

Robert Blake for Beretta

Top Ten Ways to Drive Donald Trump Insane

1. Show up to the morning meeting wearing a T-shirt that says "Don't get mad. Get everything."
2. Set him up on a blind date with Martha Stewart.
3. Take a set of shears to his hair in the middle of the night and blame it on the Combover Fairy.
4. Tell him he's fired.
5. Casually mention that Rosie O'Donnell has a nicer Rolls Royce than he does.
6. Send him a note saying "the rabbit died," and demand several million in hush money.
7. Find a loophole in his current prenup.
8. Tell him that his newly crowned Miss USA is actually a man.
9. Ask him how much he paid for his hair plugs.
10. Accidentally call him The Ronald McDonald.

Stupid Says . . .

❝I think that the film Clueless was very deep. I think it was deep in the way that it was very light. I think lightness has to come from a very deep place if it's true lightness.❞

—Alicia Silverstone

Nitwit Neuroses

Swagaphobia:
Fear of televangelism

Demiphobia:
Fear of strippers

Hillaphobia:
Fear of Southern drawls

OJaphobia:
Fear of confessions

Actors from Hell

A few famous singers have successfully crossed over into the acting realm. Frank Sinatra didn't have a problem. Neither did Bette Midler, David Bowie, or Mark Wahlberg. Cher won an Oscar for *Moonstruck,* and Will Smith is still in the Oscar hunt. But others should have thought twice before torturing us. Courtney Love, Tupac Shakur, Whitney Houston, Jessica Simpson, Eminem, Ice Cube, Jon Bon Jovi, and even Prince did their best thespian impressions. But that's not the worst of it. Madonna's *Shanghai Surprise* is less pleasant than Montezuma's revenge. Britney Spears turn in *Crossroads* will give you shingles before you can say the word "Razzie." And Mariah Carey's *Glitter* is a common torture method used in Siberian gulags.

And while we're at it, let us also pay homage to the insanely daft supermodels who decided to become "actors." Cindy Crawford's *Fair Game*, Rachel Hunter's *Larva*, Kathy Ireland's *Alien from L.A.*, Anna Nicole Smith in *Skyscraper*, Christie Brinkley in *Vegas Vacation*, and Fabio in everything he's ever done. Let it be said, for the love of all things human, please don't quit your day jobs.

The Name Game

If these celebs had gotten together!

Mark Hamill and David Hockney =
Hamhock

Wesley Snipes and Helen Hunt = Snipehunt

Stephen King and Queen Latifah =
KingnQueen

Whoopi Goldberg, Dee Dee Pfeiffer, and
Dougray Scott = WhoopDeeDo

Cruisin' for a Bruisin'

A jolly young Brit named Hugh
Had decided one night he was blue
But his date was Divine
And despite paying a fine
His rap sheet he'll never undo!

Deep Thoughts

If Sean John Puff Daddy P. Diddy Combs
decided on a permanent name, would it be
"Who Gives a Diddley?"

Royal Blunders

Prince Edward, the Earl of Wessex, is the youngest of Queen Elizabeth's children and currently spends his royal time concentrating on public duties befitting a member of the Royal Family. But that wasn't always the case. In the early 1990s, Edward formed a television production company, Ardent Television, cranking out documentaries and dramas about various royal families in Europe. In 1991, the Prince's production company tailed his nephew, Prince William at the University of St. Andrews in Scotland in the expectation of filming a gripping narrative of the young prince's escapades during his student years.

Apparently, Prince Edward thought himself unaffected by an agreement between the Royal Family and the rest of the media in the United Kingdom to leave the children, both William and Harry, alone during their school years. Buckingham Palace caught wind of the proceedings and put a stop to the production, demanding that Edward hand over every piece of footage he'd shot. So much for nepotism. Prince Edward resigned his position with the company a year later. Poor little rich royal . . . nothing to do but spend taxpayer dollars.

HOW MANY DIVAS DOES IT TAKE TO CHANGE A LIGHT BULB?

FIVE: ONE TO SCREW IT INAND FOUR OTHERS TO BERATE HER FOR NOT CALLING AN ELECTRICIAN

They Said *What?*

Shortly before the start of the Iraq war in 2003 the infamous "Chicks" weren't whistling Dixie. During a London concert, Dixie Chicks lead singer Natalie Maines pronounced that they were "ashamed that the President of the United States is from Texas." What ensued was a tornado of controversy that seriously damaged the Chicks' reputation. Despite Maine's apology, CDs were destroyed, radio stations boycotted, awards weren't won, and the funds stopped rolling in. By 2006, Maine's had retracted her apology and the Chicks began their Accidents & Accusations tour. During that same time frame, Maines and the Chicks also had a longstanding feud with country singer Toby Keith over his song "Courtesy of the Red, White & Blue," which Maines said was ignorant, and "makes country music sound ignorant." At the 2003 ACM Awards, Maines sported the acronym F.U.T.K. on her T-shirt which allegedly stood for "Friends United in Truth and Kindness." Keith later went on a talk show wearing a shirt bearing a similar sentiment. That same year, Keith publicly declared he would no longer feud with the Chicks, but it didn't seem to hurt their future artistry or controversy. At the 2007 Grammy's, the Chicks cleaned up, winning all five of the top awards.

Jailbirds

Gus Van Sant, director of notable films such as *Drugstore Cowboy* and *Good Will Hunting,* was pulled over by Portland, Oregon cops in 2006 for cruising the streets after dark with his headlights off. Bad move. Van Sant was hauled in for a mug shot and booking after a blood alcohol test proved he had a level of 0.19 percent, well over twice the state's legal limit of 0.08.

Van Sant plead "not guilty" in a court appearance, which is a shrewd move for first time offenders in Oregon. The plea entitled him to enter the state's alcohol diversion program, which effectively sidesteps the threat of a driver's license suspension, jail time, or having to perform community service. By completing the program, which includes an evaluation and alcohol related classes, Van Sant also ducked having a DUI conviction entered into his driving record. So apparently, if tests proved that Van Sant did it but he said he didn't do it, he can go to classes to teach himself to stop doing what he said he didn't do. For all our sakes, let's hope the *Drugstore Cowboy* doesn't fall off the wagon again.

Nitwit Neuroses

Mariahaphobia:
Fear of I.Q. tests

Toriaphobia:
Fear of poverty

Baldwinophobia:
Fear of voice mail

Poshaphobia:
Fear of eating disorders

Deep Thoughts

Now that *N'Sync broke up, shouldn't they
be called Out of Sync?

Stupid Says . . .

"Too many OB/GYNs aren't able to practice their love with women all across the country.**"**

—George W. Bush

Just Say Duh!

A number of cinema celebrities have created cottage industries out of their propensities for getting into idiotic altercations, but few have the consistency and apparent ferocity of superstar Russell Crowe.

Those who'd had enough of his tantrums had plenty to crow about in 2002 when he took a thrashing in a slugfest with New Zealand tycoon Eric Watson in a posh London restaurant. Crowe apparently made some disparaging cracks to Watson, the owner of a New Zealand rugby club, about the overall quality of the Kiwi team. According to one onlooker, the ensuing brawl was "a beauty." The gladiator once again got himself the proverbial thumbs down, along with a good butt kicking.

Alas, it doesn't stop there. The audacious Aussie's most infamous outburst occurred in New York in 2005 when he smacked a Mercer Hotel concierge in the chops with a telephone handset after having trouble calling his home in Australia to wish his son nighty-night. Obviously, he was just as upset as the rest of us about the price of long distance calls and the ever-growing terminally mysterious Universal Connectivity charge.

On the Web

Katie Holmes
www.stepfordwife.org

Nicole Richie
www.overeatersanonymous.org

Mel Gibson
www.imsobusted.com

Rush Limbaugh
www.passtheoxy.org

Oh Baby!

We all know that musicians are creative folks, and that certainly applies when naming their progeny. Duran Duran frontman Simon Le Bon and his wife, Yasmin Parvaneh settled on Saffron Sahara and Tullulah Pine for two of their daughters. His former bandmate, bassist John Taylor and his ex-wife Amanda De Cadenet named their daughter Atlanta Noo (short for noodlehead), and as if there wasn't enough insanity in the Jackson family, Jermaine Jackson actually named his son Jermajesty. Everyone please take a moment to curtsy.

Wedded Miss

Let it be said, that multiple marriages aren't just for the ladies. Legendary bandleader Artie Shaw was hitched eight times, once to Lana Turner (who herself married eight times) and also to Ava Gardner. Mickey Rooney, who was also married to Ava Gardner for two years in the 1940s, has had eight wives. And talk show legend Larry King, producer Robert Evans, and comedian Stan Laurel have each pranced down the aisle seven times. Any chance you get a discount on flowers after the sixth wedding?

Pimp My Ride

Madonna:
Pontiac Vibrator

Mickey Rourke:
Nissan Bath Finder

Sylvester Stallone:
Ferrari Testosterossa

Jerry Seinfeld:
VW Rabbi

Viral VIPs

Match the celeb with their computer virus:

a. Dan Quayle   **f.** Simon Cowell
b. Jennifer Lopez   **g.** Rosie O'Donnell
c. Jessica Simpson   **h.** Karen Carpenter
d. Al Gore   **i.** Tori Spelling
e. Ozzy Osbourne   **j.** Michael Jackson

1. Whenever you enter a password it asks you if you're aware of a 9/11 conspiracy.

2. If you run a virus check, your nose falls off.

3. Ever time you type the word "mother" your computer asks you for money.

4. All of your desktop icons have turned into pictures of Ryan Seacrest.

5. If you type "world's worst movies" into Yahoo it takes you directly to the *Gigli* Web site.

6. If you hit delete your machine starts screaming half-slurred epithets at you.

7. When you run spellcheck the word "potatoe" comes up as correct.

8. Whenever you eject a disk your computer makes a puking sound.

9. When you open your browser it asks you to pay homage to the Internet inventor.

10. When your aquarium screen saver kicks in it asks you to identify the Chicken of the Sea.

Answers: 1-g, 2-j, 3-i, 4-f, 5-b, 6-e, 7-a, 8-h, 9-d, 10-c

Jokers and Trout Pouts

It's no secret that many celebs opt for a nip and tuck now and again. Most times the changes are so subtle that they simply appear refreshed. Other times, not so much. When it comes to facial enhancement, there's no sense dwelling on Michael Jackson, because whether we admit it or not, we're all just waiting for gravity to take what's left of his schnozz. Other celebs, however, have piqued our interest because their faces have suddenly taken on the frozen Joker look, the terminally surprised look, or the frighteningly popular "walking in a wind tunnel" look. Joan Rivers, Burt Reynolds, Marie Osmond, and Mickey Rourke are just a few of the many celebs who've attempted to cheat time—and it doesn't stop there. A bevy of beauties have gone under the knife to enhance their cleavage, suck fat out of everywhere, and regularly inject their lips to create the ultimate trout pout. Why, you ask? Everybody wants perfection in an imperfect world. But let's face it—it's only a matter of time before the fountain of youth dries up, and in twenty years there will be more droopy hooters, saggy lips, and dragging hips than you can shake a stick at. Seriously, would you really want to inject yourself with something that has the word "tox" in it?

Model Behavior

In this life we have genuinely talented actors, wannabe actors, and those who are under the permanent delusion that they actually have a speck of acting ability. Supermodels, as we've already learned, primarily fall into the latter category. You hope, however, that perhaps they're not just pretty faces—that in fact, there's something more to them than a thong and a grin. Guess again.

❝Because modeling is lucrative, I'm able to save up and be more particular about the acting roles I take.❞
—Kathy Ireland, star of Alien from L.A.

❝Mick Jagger and I just really liked each other a lot. We talked all night. We had the same views on nuclear disarmament.❞
—Jerry Hall

❝I make a lot of money, but I don't want to talk about that. I work very hard and I'm worth every cent.❞
—Naomi Campbell

❝I've always thought Marilyn Monroe looked fabulous, but I'd kill myself if I was that fat.❞
—Elizabeth Hurley

❝I don't get out of bed for less than $10,000 a day.❞
—Linda Evangelista

WHY DID JESSICA SIMPSON
CROSS THE ROAD?

SHE FIGURED THE
CHICKEN
**WAS REALLY A TUNA
AND WOULD JUST SWIM
OUT OF HER WAY**

Flying the Overly Friendly Skies

Exclusive membership in the "mile-high club" is more an issue of bragging rights than joining, say, the local chapter of 4-H. Mere mortals can, and often do, get away with mid-air antics with fellow passengers taking little or no notice at all. If a celeb engages in such a tête-a-tête, however, things can get a bit dicey. In 2007, A-lister Ralph Fiennes applied for mile-high status during a Qantas Air flight from Australia to India. Apparently, flight attendant Lisa Robertson engaged in a bit of banter with Fiennes and finally "couldn't control myself." The urge allegedly led her to a private make-out session and subsequently, a bodice ripping and unprotected Harlequin encounter in the loo. Fiennes didn't put up a struggle, but was obviously thinking with the wrong head. The romp didn't go unnoticed, and Robertson later lost her job. Fiennes continued on his journey to India, where he was acting as an ambassador to UNICEF to promote STD awareness and safe sex. Oh the irony. Perhaps next time Fiennes will keep his carry-on luggage carefully stowed.

Favorite Movies of the Truly Daft

Francis Ford Coppola: Planet of the Grapes

Ted Kennedy: Crouching Tiger,
Hidden Flagon

K.D. Lang: Must Love Clogs

Paris Hilton: Love is a Many
Splendored Ring

Anna Nicole Smith films that were never released:

- From Here to Paternity
- How to Marry a Billionaire
- Sleeping Duty
- If There's a Will, There's a Way
- Who's Afraid of Virgie Arthur?
- Die Hard with Attendants
- Pride and Intelligence
- The Wizard of Odds
- Drs. Doolittle
- Gentlemen Prefer Bonds
- sex, lies and videosnake
- Terminator 4: Judgment Daze
- Send in the Clowns

Diva Darlings—Not!

It's likely there are only a few humans on planet earth who haven't heard the term "Bennifer." They were, of course, the unlikely duo of Ben Affleck and Jennifer Lopez. Doomed from the start, theirs was a rather sordid show of bling and Bentleys. What isn't as well known is that Jenny from the Block has been around the block more than once. Current hubby Marc Anthony is her third and longest lasting hubby. In 1997, J. Lo married Cuban waiter Ojani Noa, a pairing that lasted only a year. In 2001, La Lopez gave it another shot and married Cris Judd, a former backup dancer. After a year, the honeymoon sunk faster than *Gigli* ticket sales.

Nitwit Neuroses

Abdulophobia:
Fear of live interviews

Stoneaphobia:
Fear of *Basic Instinct* sequels

Schwarzenegaphobia:
Fear of groping

Woodyallephobia:
Fear of Polaroids

Leave a Message!

Mel Gibson:
(In Aramaic). *This is Max. I'm mad. They're all after me. I'm just a good little altar boy. The voices are telling me to move to Iceland. It's safe there. And it's cold. If you hear this, board the next plane to Reykjavik. Bring plenty of Budweiser. I'll be waiting.*

Bumper Snickers!

BE NICE TO YOUR KIDS. THEY'LL CHOOSE YOUR NURSING HOME.
Judge Judy

DON'T TREAT ME ANY DIFFERENTLY THAN YOU WOULD THE QUEEN.
Mariah Carey

They Said *What?*

One of the great legendary Hollywood feuds of all time was between starlets Bette Davis and Joan Crawford, and although they worked for different studios (Crawford at MGM Studios and Davis at Warner Bros.), that didn't stop them from engaging in a long-term rivalry fueled by extreme jealousy. Davis apparently wished she had Crawford's glamorous image and Crawford was envious of Davis' acting ability and her impressive number of Oscar nominations. There was also a romantic rivalry for Franchot Tone—Davis was interested in him but he was dating Crawford. The two divas first worked together in 1962 filming *What Ever Happened to Baby Jane?*, a thriller about sisterly rivalry. Though they both had careers on the line and were professional on the set, Davis was quoted as saying: "The best time I ever had with Joan in a film was when I pushed her down the stairs in *What Ever Happened to Baby Jane?*" When Davis was nominated for an Oscar for her role in the movie, Crawford campaigned against her. The bad blood continued until their deaths. Crawford died in 1977 and Davis in 1989.

The Name Game

If these celebs had gotten together!

Carly Simon and Dennis Hopper = Carhop

Michael Crichton and Baby Spice = Crybaby

Lil' Kim and Willie Aames = LittleWillie

Norah Jones and Biggie Smalls = Nobiggie

On the Web

P. Diddy
www.cantdecideonaname.com

Keith Urban
www.oldhabitsdiehard.com

Anne Heche
www.beammeupscotty.com

Deep Thoughts

If Lindsay Lohan married Atilla the Hun,
would she heretofore be know as
Lindsay Lohun?

HOW MANY REHABBED CELEBS
DOES IT TAKE TO CHANGE A
LIGHT BULB?

JUST ONE.
BUT IT HAS TO REALLY
WANT TO CHANGE

Jailbirds

Christian Brando, the eldest of legendary A-lister Marlon Brando's children, was by every account a troubled and violent alcoholic and drug abuser when he shot his half-sister's boyfriend to death at the Brando estate in Los Angeles in 1990. Christian's sister, Cheyenne, had reportedly woven a schizophrenic tale of physical and mental torment she suffered at the hands of boyfriend Dag Drollet—a tale that put Christian into a drunken and ultimately, homicidal rage.

Drollet was discovered moments after the shooting—by Marlon, Cheyenne, and other family members—with a bullet in the back of his head, a tobacco pouch in one hand, and the television remote control in the other. After procedural mistakes by investigating officers and Cheyenne Brando's escape to Tahiti (courtesy of her father) to avoid testifying in the case, Christian copped to a manslaughter plea deal that put him in prison for just six years. According to Christian, he had been, "just trying to scare the guy."

Excuse me? He couldn't have just snuck up on the poor fellow and yelled "boo?"

Hell Hath No Fury

One of the most notorious rock concerts in history took place at the Altamont Speedway in Northern California in 1969. Just four months after the original Woodstock festival, Altamont would prove to be the death knell of peaceful flower-powered musical gatherings the world over. Under the heading of "questionable judgment," the Rolling Stones and their road manager Sam Cutler invited the Hell's Angels motorcycle club to take care of security at the event. The result was a drug and alcohol fueled riot that left a number of concert goers beaten with pool cues and one man stabbed to death. Cutler denied that the Hell's Angels were hired to "police" the fiasco, insisting that the bikers were brought aboard only to protect the sound equipment. In hindsight, Cutler's argument seems about as rational as inviting Michael Jackson to chaperone a grade school slumber party.

Tripping Out

What do Dan Quayle and Raquel Welch have in common? Aside from the obvious fact that they're celebrities, they both appear to have a very serious problem with American history and, among other things, are severely geographically challenged. If this doesn't make your head explode—nothing will:

❝It is wonderful to be here in the great state of Chicago.**❞**

—Dan Quayle

❝I was asked to come to Chicago because Chicago is one of our fifty-two states.**❞**

—Raquel Welch

Perhaps the two of them might consider traveling with Britney Spears:

❝The cool thing about being famous is traveling. I have always wanted to travel overseas, like to Canada and stuff.**❞**

—Britney Spears

❝I've never really wanted to go to Japan. Simply because I don't like eating fish. And I know that's very popular out there in Africa.**❞**

—Britney Spears

Unholy Matrimony

Rounding out *Forbes* top ten list of celeb divorces (which would be akin to winning the lottery to us mere mortals) is terminally big-lipped crooner Mick Jagger. A Rolling Stone may gather no moss, but they do gather a host of women, children, and seemingly endless truckloads of cash. Jagger has seven children with four different mothers and continues shaking his booty on the worldwide stage to the present day. For all intents and purposes, a legal snafu got Jagger off the hook when his twenty-two year relationship with model Jerry Hall ended in 1999, after it came to light that an illicit affair produced another child. It's estimated that the settlement was somewhere between $15 to $25 million, a rather paltry sum decided upon largely by the legitimacy of their disputed Hindu wedding in Bali in 1990. Was it to Hall's satisfaction? Apparently so. The couple remain in close contact to the present day.

WHY DID MCCAULEY
C U L K I N
GET MARRIED?

HE WAS TIRED
OF BEING HOME
A L O N E

Need a Lift?

If you're a famous celeb worth bazillions of dollars, what's the last thing you're likely to do? If you answered shoplifting, you would be correct. Apparently Winona Ryder missed the memo about that one. The girl was interrupted on December 12, 2001, when she was busted for swiping over $5,500 worth of clothes and various accessories from Saks Fifth Avenue's Beverly Hills store. Apparently, this was not her first foray into the criminal world. She also took various liberties at Barneys and Neiman Marcus, but those instances didn't come into play during her sensational two-week trial. Acquitted of a burglary charge, but convicted of vandalism and felony grand theft, Ryder faced three years in the pokey. In the end, she received a strict three-year probation including over 400 hours of community service, fines, counseling, and monetary remuneration to Saks. Drug charges were dropped for the eight different painkillers she was carrying with her during her shopping spree. Wow. All this for a few bits of cloth and an $80 pair of socks. Reality bites, indeed.

Nitwit Neuroses

Kirstialliphobia:
Fear of accurate scales

Hughaphobia:
Fear of strumpets

Madonnaphobia:
Fear of Gandhi

Princephobia:
Fear of unpronounceable names

The Name Game

If these celebs had gotten together!

Cat Stevens and Kitty Carlisle = KittyCat

Fisher Stevens and Larry King = FisherKing

Hugh Jackman and Jill St. John = JacknJill

Rachel Stirling and Stephen Fry = StirFry

Room Service

The godfather of hotel room abusers is undoubtedly eccentric billionaire Howard Hughes, who checked into the Desert Inn Hotel in Las Vegas for a ten-day stay in 1966, and wound up secluded in his room for four years. During that four-year hiatus the room was never once cleaned, and Hughes fell into the bizarre habit of putting his bodily waste into jars and stacking them against the walls. When hotel management finally threatened to evict Hughes for hogging the entire top floor, Hughes simply bought the hotel. During his stay, he also bought the Silver Slipper Hotel across the street complete with its mechanical slipper facade. The toe of the slipper apparently paused and pointed toward Hughes' room before restarting its rotation, which was unnerving to the neurotic billionaire. His first command as owner was to have the rotation adjusted. Seems we should all be thankful the hotel wasn't across the street from the Mustang Ranch.

Say It Ain't So!

Products or organizations that celebs should never endorse:

Charleton Heston for PETA

Jessica Simpson for Chicken of the Sea

Lara Flynn Boyle for Botox

Mickey Rourke for Irish Spring

On the Web

Kenny Chesney
www.iamnotafraud.com

Anna Nicole Smith
www.deathbenotproud.com

Zsa Zsa Gabor
www.imarriedacheater.com

Don Imus
www.rutgersfan.org

Mix and Mingle:
Annoying Celeb Anagrams

Nick Lachey   Katie Holmes
Ben Affleck   Melanie Griffith
Winona Ryder   Carmen Electra
Eddy Murphy   Mike Tyson
Tori Spelling   Geraldo Rivera

1. MENIAL FIREFIGHT
2. DYE DRYHUMP
3. PIGEON TRILLS
4. LACE CRATERMEN
5. RADAR EGOLIVER
6. CLAN HICKEY
7. MISTAKE HOLE
8. TINY SMOKE
9. BAFFLE NECK
10. WARDEN IRONY

Answers:
1-Melanie Griffith
2-Eddy Murphy
3-Tori Spelling
4-Carmen Electra
5-Geraldo Rivera
6-Nick Lachey
7-Katie Holmes
8-Mike Tyson
9-Ben Affleck
10-Winona Ryder.

Deep Thoughts

If Brad Pitt hailed from Georgia, would
he be called a Peach Pitt?

Royal Blunders

Sarah Margaret Ferguson took the British
Royal Family by storm when she married
Prince Andrew in 1986, officially becoming
Her Royal Highness The Duchess of York.
Popularly known as "Fergie," the Duchess
turned the storm into a hurricane in 1992
when she was photographed with American
financial manager John Bryant. The surrep-
titious photos showed Bryant happily nib-
bling on the bare toes of the equally
bare-chested royal in a not-so-secret hide-
away, creating a media explosion that sig-
naled the end of Fergie's courtly lifestyle.
Officially divorced from Andrew in that
same year, Fergie toed the line by fleeing
a venomous and spiteful British press and
moving to New York.

A Hole Lotta Love

Not many folks can lay claim to having been married to a dead rock star, and most of 'em manage to go on leading fairly low-key existences. Priscilla Presley, Yoko Ono, Paula Yates, and James Brown's dozen or so widows aren't everyday tabloid fodder. The same isn't true, however, of our dear uber-grunge queen Courtney Love, widow of Nirvana's Kurt Cobain who made a date with a shotgun in 1994. For the next decade, Love indulged in the typical sex, drugs, and rock n' roll lifestyle that ultimately sent her husband over the edge. The rollercoaster continues, but fortunately Love is leaning toward a healthier and less chaotic lifestyle. Nonetheless, her words remain on the record:

❝But let me tell you something. Gloria Steinem never helped me out; Larry Flynt did.❞

❝What makes the most money for this business? Dead rock stars.❞

❝If you want to ask about my drug problem, go ask my big, fat, smart, ten-pound daughter, she'll answer any questions you have about it.❞

❝Thank you very much, your honor.❞

WHAT DID GOD SAY AFTER CREATING
PEE WEE HERMAN?

I CAN DO BETTER

Jailbirds

Former *Baywatch* babe Yasmine Bleeth, who has been featured in a number of national magazines, added to her pictorial resume with a rather unflattering mug shot taken in a Michigan police station after being arrested for possession of drug paraphernalia and cocaine in 2001. The beachbabe-gone-bad agreed to a plea bargain and received a two-year probationary sentence along with 100 hours of community service. Bleeth satisfied the terms of her legal arrangement in 2004, and after a couple of stints in the uber-spendy Promises rehab facility, she has by all accounts remained free of narcotic enticements. The nearly unrecognizable mugshot, however, will forever remain in the celebrity jailbird hall of shame.

Oh Baby!

No one wants their kid to get teased relentlessly throughout their formative years. Ben Affleck and Jennifer Garner's little gal Violet is likely safe, as is Meg Ryan's Daisy, and Jude Law and Sadie Frost's daughter Iris. But what about Rachel Griffith's son Banjo? Or musician Melanie Blatt's daughter Lilyella? Gary Oldman's son Gulliver? Suri Cruise? Coco Arquette? Or John Malkovich's daughter Amandine? Seriously. That's almost criminal. No one should be named after a green bean casserole.

Leave a Message!

James Cameron:
You've reached Jim. Can't come to the phone at present. I'm out searching for Atlantis. Then I'll be revealing the contents of Cleopatra's lost tomb, the exact location of Bigfoot, the Holy Grail, and the Loch Ness Monster, which I've currently got chained to my swimming pool. Oh . . . and I've got the guy who shot J.F.K. Have a nice day, Philistines.

Stud Farming

Heidi Fleiss (pronounced "F-lice"), the notorious Hollywood madam who spent twenty-one months in the clink for tax evasion and money laundering, is on another fast track to infamy with the planned opening of a Nevada brothel, tentatively called The Stud Farm. Fleiss' idea is to open a sort of "dog house" in counterpoint to the ubiquitous cat houses of Nevada, where she will cater to wealthy, seriously bored women who are willing to pay for services by a staff of gorgeous gigolos.

The Stud Farm is expected to be built on a patch of cactus owned by Fleiss that is—in her own words—"in the middle of the middle of nowhere." Fleiss is still seeking county approval for her venture, and will also require a little cooperation from the state legislature. Current statutes in Nevada that regulate prostitution are written specifically for female brothel professionals. As the law is now written, Fleiss' pretty boys would be required to undergo monthly examinations by a gynecologist. How do you like them stirrups?

Bumper Snickers!

I'M OUT OF ESTROGEN AND I HAVE A GUN.
Roseanne Barr

CAUTION: YOUR DAUGHTER MIGHT
BE ONBOARD.
Kevin Federline

Favorite Movies of the Truly Daft

Mariah Carey: Breakfast, Lunch, and Dinner at Tiffany's

Jimmy Swaggart: Sense and Repentability

Naomi Campbell: When a Stranger Crawls

Lindsay Lohan: Last of the Mojitos

Wedded Miss

In 2001, actor Robert Blake found himself in a world of hurt when he was accused of murdering his wife Bonny Lee Bakley, and was subsequently acquitted of the crime in 2005. Tragic as the situation was, it brought to light Bakley's history of celebrity obsession and her issue of being a serial husband seeker. Bakley was apparently married an astonishing ten times, though most of the unions didn't last long. Nonetheless, she had four children, the last of whom was a daughter who she claimed might have been Christian Brando's but ultimately turned out to be Blake's. Her horrid murder notwithstanding, after hoofing it to altar ten times you've really gotta wonder how many crock pots that woman owned, don't you?

Deep Thoughts

If Milli Vanilli and Vanilla Ice bought a Baskin Robbins, would they rename it Vanilli Vanilla?

Stupid Says . . .

❝If you want to say it with flowers, a single rose says: 'I'm cheap!'**❞**

—Delta Burke

Top Ten Ways to Drive Paris Hilton Insane

1. Take away her cell phone.
2. Tell her that you stay at Motel 6.
3. Suggest she start dating someone worth less than $100 million.
4. Refuse to serve her sushi on the grounds that it's insulting to the fish who gave their lives.
5. Make her take a driving test.
6. Hire her for a show called *The Difficult Life*.
7. Inform her that BFF stands for Big Financial Fraud.
8. Tell her that Hermes has gone out of business.
9. Ask her where Canada is.
10. Force her to read this book.

Hair Today, Gone Tomorrow

Not since Delilah cut Samson's locks has someone's hairdo been so coveted as Keri Russell's was in her hit show *Felicity*. In 1998, Russell burst onto the small screen, her long luxurious curls becoming her character's crowning glory and the envy of women the world over. So good an actress was Russell that after *Felicity's* first season, she captured a Golden Globe. In August of 1999, however, Russell chopped off her trademark locks, and all hell broke loose. Though it couldn't be confirmed that the show's move to a different night or Russell's new short coif caused a huge ratings drop, it nonetheless enraged *Felicity* fans. As a result, WB network bigwigs set new standards which stated that any cast member's hairstyle change required executive approval. Felicity managed to stay on the tube until 2002, but the outrage over an innocent haircut lingered. What do you suppose would've happened if Ross had taken a pair of friendly shears to Rachel's long locks?

He Said, She Said

And speaking of Rachel, no discussion of Hollywood breakups would be complete without Jennifer and Brad. When Aniston and Pitt married in 2000 they became instant Hollywood royalty. How could there be a more perfect match than these two genetically blessed people? They were the golden couple of movie stardom and as such, were constant targets of the media and tabloids. For years, there was worldwide anticipation of a baby Pitt and fairytale happily-ever-after storyline—but fate intervened. The world was shocked when the couple that had been put so high on a pedestal announced their separation in January of 2005, and the tabloids had a field day speculating that Jen didn't want a baby and Brad was having a fling with Angelina Jolie, his co-star in *Mr. & Mrs. Smith*. Neither turned out to be true, although pictures of Pitt and Jolie together started surfacing in April 2005, a mere one month after Aniston filed for divorce, and shortly thereafter Jolie became pregnant with Pitt's child. On the whole, it appeared to be an amicable divorce, although in a now infamous *Vanity Fair* article, Aniston said of her ex: "There's a sensitivity chip that's missing."

Pimp My Ride

Tom Arnold:
Pontiac Trans Ham

O.J. Simpson:
Nissan Strangler

Michael Jackson:
Ford Bronchitis

Bill Clinton:
Cadillac Escalaid

Last Breath

In 1998, actor Woody Harrelson jumped on an air-headed trend by opening a health food restaurant and oxygen bar in Hollywood, California, brilliantly named "O2." The oxygen bar concept seemed likely to suffocate on its own stupidity, but still managed to sputter into the first years of 2000 with establishments popping up in urban areas all over the country. Throughout the recent history of the fad, the general public recognized the general silliness of oxygen bars, and stayed away from them in droves. Harrelson's O2 bar saw a wild but short-lived success triggered by media attention, and has since quietly disappeared into thin air.

WHAT DO MEL GIBSON AND A
BEER BOTTLE
HAVE IN COMMON?

THEY'RE BOTH
E M P T Y
FROM THE NECK UP.

The Name Game

If these celebs had gotten together!

Martin Short and Robert Stack = Shortstack

John Ratzenberger and Joan Rivers =
RiverRat

Margo Kidder and Kanye West = GoWest

Goldie Hawn, Keanu Reeves, and Wolfgang
Puck = HawkeePuck

Deep Thoughts

If Godzilla is an atheist, does he have
to change his name?

Stupid Says . . .

❝I'm so naive about finances. Once when
my mother mentioned an amount and I
realized that I didn't understand she had
to explain: 'That's like three Mercedes.'
Then I understood.❞

—Brooke Shields

Bumper Snickers!

MY MOTHER IS A TRAVEL AGENT
FOR GUILT TRIPS.
Melissa Rivers

HAVE YOU SHEEN MY EX-HUSBAND?
Denise Richards

Nitwit Neuroses

Travoltaphobia:
Fear of Sweathogs

Celinaophobia:
Fear of *Titanic* soundtracks

Trendaphobia:
Fear of Bobby Trendy outfits

Whitnephobia:
Fear of crack

I Scream, You Scream . . .

Match the celeb with their favorite ice cream

Jerry Seinfeld   Mel Gibson
Oprah Winfrey   Prince
Elizabeth Taylor   Martha Stewart
Keanu Reeves   Sylvester Stallone
Nicole Richie   Jesse James

1. Rocky Roadkill
2. Pralines 'n Scream
3. Spewmoni
4. The ice cream formerly known as Pistachio
5. Wreath Bar Crunch
6. Chocolate Cheap
7. Rainbow Surebutt
8. Wrench Vanilla
9. Cat on a Hot Tin Roof Sundae
10. Neopolitan

Answers:
1-Sylvester Stallone.
2-Mel Gibson.
3-Nicole Richie.
4-Prince.
5-Martha Stewart.
6-Jerry Seinfeld.
7-Oprah Winfrey.
8-Jesse James.
9-Elizabeth Taylor.
10-Keanu Reeves.

Are You There God, It's Me—Anne

Sadly, many celebs are known more for their bizarre behavior or their flawed existences than they are their acting ability. Just spend a few minutes studying former Reservoir Dog Tom Sizemore, or the trainwreck that was diet pill diva Anna Nicole Smith. Anne Heche is no slouch in the thespian department, but her name didn't become a household fave because of her acting chops. The waifish blonde is perhaps best known for being the former Mrs. Ellen DeGeneres, and for her highly publicized mental breakdown in 2000 after the two parted company—a breakdown that found her aimlessly roaming about in rural Fresno, California. Can you imagine the look on that family's face, when they opened the door to their farmhouse and found a drug-induced Heche on their stoop claiming her name was Celestia, that she was God's daughter, and that a spaceship was coming to take her to heaven? Allegedly clad in shorts and a bra, Heche apparently asked if she could take a shower. Alrighty then. Definitely something you don't see every day.

Be warned: The next time your doorbell rings, take a deep breath. It may not be the Avon Lady calling.

Tom Cruise sequels that were never released:

- Missionaries Impossible
- Top Grunge
- Bars of the Worlds
- Vanilla Skydiving
- Born on the Sixth of July
- Frisky Business
- Days of Blunder
- Pain Man
- The Color of Honey
- All the Left Moves
- A Few Good Women
- Eyes Permanently Shut

Favorite Movies of the Truly Daft

Kevin Federline: Goodbye, Mrs. Chips

Geraldo Rivera: Broadcast Snooze

Tori Spelling: Children of a Lesser Snob

Wayne Newton: The Sound of Muzak

Jailbirds

With a history of sketchy behavior and drug and alcohol abuse, Christian Slater has been a tabloid mainstay for years. Slater's most serious run-in with the law occurred in Los Angeles in 1997, when he was arrested for assault with a deadly weapon and battery. Reportedly jacked-up on heroin at a party, Slater punched out his one-time girlfriend, fashion editor Michelle Jonas, and then actually bit a brave soul who came to her defense. When the cops were called to the scene, Slater attacked the officers and got himself handcuffed and hauled off to the hoosegow. Felony charges against him were eventually dropped, but he was sentenced to three months in the county slammer.

In 2003, Slater was married to actress Ryan Haddon when she fulfilled a sort of Karmic destiny by beaning Slater with a highball glass in Las Vegas, sending him to the ER for twenty well-earned stitches. Slater is currently seeking a divorce from Haddon, claiming spousal abuse. Who's he kidding? Pot, meet kettle.

Harsh Reality

If you're a celebrity couple, what's the last thing in the world you should do? If reality show is your answer than you would be correct. A few families have managed to keep their members intact, namely the Osbourne gang and Gene Simmons and his *Family Jewels*. Many others however, have fallen victim to the reality couple's divorce curse. The most recent victim is red-headed rehabbed Partridge alum Danny Bonaduce and his wife Gretchen. Their show, *Breaking Bonaduce* was a trainwreck in progress, much of it focusing on Bonaduce's struggles with alcohol and a host of other no-nos. Married in 1990, they filed for divorce in 2007. On the same dissolution track were Travis Barker and Shanna Moakler, whose show *Meet the Barkers* didn't stop them from filing for the big "D" in 2007. Of course, we all know that Britney and Kevin: *Chaotic* didn't have a happy ending. The same goes for Carmen Electra and Dave Navarro's 2004 effort *Til Death Do Us Part: Carmen and Dave*. They also filed for divorce in 2007. And who could forget (or would love to forget) *Newlyweds: Nick and Jessica*, a show so painful it made your teeth hurt.

Nitwit Neuroses

Cheneyaphobia:
Fear of duck hunting

Federphobia:
Fear of bald women

Aguileraphobia:
Fear of Mousketeers

Diazaphobia:
Fear of acting classes

Bumper snickers!

MY OTHER CAR IS A BROOM.
Anne Coulter

I'M HEADED HOME. MY VILLAGE IS
MISSING ITS IDIOT.
Don Imus

Just Say Duh!

The parable of the Good Samaritan was reinvented in the wee hours of the morning on Los Angeles' Santa Monica Boulevard by neighborly Eddie Murphy when he stopped to "help out" a mini-skirted transvestite hooker named Atisone Seiuli. True to the altruistic spirit of the tale, Murphy gave Seiuli a few shekels and kindly offered to provide her a room at the inn. Of course the story doesn't end there. Murphy and his foundling passenger were pulled over by Los Angeles County Sheriff's deputies, who spent half an hour gushing over Murphy and pleading for autographs before arresting Seiuli on an outstanding prostitution violation. The story quickly hit the tabloids, and inventive transvestite hookers began peddling sordid Murphy encounters all over Los Angeles. Several of Murphy's explanations regarding his caring nature included: "I'm just being a nice guy, and "I've seen hookers on corners . . . I'll pull over," and the ever popular: "I'll empty my wallet to help out." Given the circumstances, it's perhaps best to quote a familiar source. As Shrek pointed out: "people judge me before they know me." Lucky for Eddy that in this instance *he* didn't have to face the judge.

Viral VIPs

Match the celeb with their computer virus:

a. Billy Ray Cyrus   **e.** Tonya Harding
b. Pee Wee Herman   **f.** Tom Cruise
c. Kirstie Alley   **g.** David Hasselhoff
d. Janet Jackson   **h.** Russell Crowe

1. If you attempt to stop a program from loading your computer cracks your knee cap.
2. If you hit the wrong keys it reminds you to go to your AA meeting.
3. If you can't access the Internet you suddenly throw your phone at a co-worker.
4. Whenever a porno ad pops up it claims that it's just a wardrobe malfunction.
5. If you sit in front of the machine too long it tells you to get off your achy breaky butt.
6. Whenever you hit the control key, you have the overwhelming urge to jump on your couch.
7. When you attempt to access an X-rated Web site, a vice cop taps you on the shoulder.
8. If you type too much, a message comes up asking if you've called Jenny yet.

Answers: 1-e, 2-g, 3-h, 4-d, 5-a, 6-f, 7-b, 8-c

Stupid Says . . .

❝I'm using my brain for the first time in a long time.**❞**
— Victoria "Posh Spice" Beckham

Unholy Matrimony

It's fair to say that Hollywood legend Elizabeth Taylor is no schlump in the matrimony department. Giving Zsa Zsa a run for the money, Liz has been hitched eight times, her ex-entourage including Michael Wilding, Michael Todd, Eddie Fisher, John Warner, Larry Fortensky, and Richard Burton, whom she married and divorced twice. Taylor's first husband, Nicholas Conrad Hilton Jr. was actually the son of Zsa Zsa Gabor's second husband, Conrad Sr., a fact that means Taylor is also related by marriage to Paris Hilton. Kevin Bacon is twitching uncontrollably as we speak.

On the Web

Al Gore
www.theinternetismine.com

Jennifer Lopez
www.thereisnoexcuseforgigli.com

Jennifer Grey
www.ignoremynose.org

Michael Jackson
www.babieslovebalconies.com

Deep Thoughts

If you named your daughter Apple, why wouldn't you name your son Orange?

Dude Looks Like My Baby!

If someone asked you what the blockbuster trilogy *Lord of the Rings* and the rock band Aerosmith had in common, the last thing you'd think of is genetics. But if you did, you'd be right. Liv Tyler, who played the part of Arwen in all three *Lord of the Rings* films and was one of *People* magazine's fifty most beautiful people in 1997, was raised by her mother Bebe Buell with help from rock star Todd Rundgren, whom Liv believed to be her natural father. In 1986, at the age of nine, she discovered that Steven Tyler of the legendary rock and roll band Aerosmith, was actually her biological father. The revelation struck Liv after seeing a concert and noticing a family resemblance. Her genetics had originally been hidden from both her and her father because of Tyler's self-destructive drug intake during the first years of her life. The dark-haired, big-lipped beauty changed her name from Liv Rundgren to Liv Tyler soon after learning the truth, and with Tyler's eventual success in drug rehab, the pair were finally reunited. Dream on!

DID YOU HEAR ABOUT
WOODY ALLEN'S
LATEST MOVIE?

IT'S CALLED HONEY,
I MARRIED THE KIDS

Hang 'em High

Where does one begin with Michael Jackson? Well, there's his radical change of appearance from Jackson Fiver to "Barely Aliver," the ever-present surgical masks, his procuring the so-called Elephant Man's bones, the oxygen tank, marrying Lisa Marie Presley, and a host of sordid accusations, settlements, and trials for inappropriate behavior. The public will never know what is true. So be it. But there is one incredible act of stupidity that's well recorded.

The King of Pop's bonehead move of the decade came in Berlin in 2002, when he was in town to accept a humanitarian award. At his hotel, in response to a screaming horde of fans, Jackson actually lifted his youngest son, Prince Michael II (aka "Blanket") over the balcony railing and briefly dangled him over the edge. The act of lunacy was a true abomination, one that the Wacko Wonder did apologize for, citing he "made a terrible mistake," and that he'd "never intentionally endanger the lives of my children." Hmm. Wouldn't intentionally endanger them, but hangs one over a balcony? Sounds a bit like an if-the-glove-don't-fit-you-must-acquit excuse, doesn't it?

I See Drunk People

Child actor Haley Joel Osment, who will forever be saddled with parodies of his memorable "I see dead people" line in M. Night Shamalyan's *The Sixth Sense,* was alone when he wrecked his car in July of 2006. The cause of the crash was, no doubt, his blood alcohol level which was twice the legal limit in California. Osment escaped spending the night in the pokey given that he suffered a fractured rib and shoulder blade, and instead went to the hospital. As a result of his driving debacle, he was sentenced to three years probation, sixty hours of alcohol rehab, and a $1,500 fine. It is hoped that in real life, Osment is now seeing more sober people.

Stupid Says . . .

❝I want to wait to have sex until I'm married.❞

—Britney Spears

Bumper Snickers!

HOW'S MY DRIVING?
CALL 1-800-KISS-MY-HINEY.
Simon Cowell

I FOUND JESUS. HE'S BEEN HIDING IN
THE BASEMENT ALL THESE YEARS.
Jimmy Swaggart

Leave a Message!

James Gandolfini:
*It's Gandolfini. Leave a message. Live or
die. Your choice.*

The Name Game

If these celebs had gotten together!

Mia Hamm and Ryan O'Neal = HamnRy

Whitney Houston and Charlie Watts = HouWatt?

Fred Astaire and Roma Downey = StairDown

Sylvester Stallone, Gary Oldman, and Foxy Brown = SlyOldFox

Royal Blunders

In case you're wondering, there is no end to the absolute stupidity that is Prince Philip. On a 1994 trip to the Cayman Islands, a territory of Great Britain, Prince Philip made a side trip to the Cayman Islands National Museum. While there, he asked the curator of the museum, "Aren't most of you descended from pirates?"

WHAT DOES
BRITNEY SPEARS
SAY WHEN YOU BLOW IN HER EAR?

THANKS FOR THE
R E F I L L !

Wedded Miss

One of the worst marriages on record has to be that of Liza Minnelli and David Gest. Married in 2002 at a service that featured Elizabeth Taylor as the maid of honor and Michael Jackson as best man, the pairing was doomed from the words "I do." The wedding photos alone were enough to frighten children and small animals. Just over a year later the couple separated, and the accusations started to fly into the great unknown. Gest filed suit for spousal abuse and thankfully, their planned reality show never came to fruition. In this instance we can all blame Jacko, because he's the one who introduced the "happy" couple. Well done on the matchmaking, Wacko!

Bumper Snickers!

I'M AS CONFUSED AS A BABY
IN A TOPLESS BAR!
Hugh Hefner

DYSLEXIC SATAN WORSHIPPERS BELIEVE
THEY'RE WORSHIPPING SANTA
Pat Robertson

Stupid Says . . .

"If Michelle Pfeiffer gave Mel Gibson a vial of blood to wear around his neck in a movie you'd think it was terribly romantic, everyone would cry and they'd win awards. But in real life if someone does that they'd be considered weird.**"**

—Billy Bob Thornton on his wearing a vial of blood from then-wife Angelina Jolie

Nitwit Neuroses

Brookaphobia:
Fear of Tom Cruise

Couricophobia:
Fear of perkiness

Regiphobia:
Fear of Kelly Ripa

Lenophobia:
Fear of jutting chins

Jailbirds

Tracey Gold, best known for her stint on the situation comedy *Growing Pains* in the 1980s, was arrested in 2004 for driving under the influence after crashing the family SUV with her husband and their three children aboard. Her husband, Roby Marshall, and two of the three kids sustained injuries, none of which were life-threatening. Blair Clark, Gold's publicist, reportedly denied that the arrest had taken place, and that reports from the California Highway Patrol had been greatly exaggerated. But Gold eventually gave up the act and pled guilty to charges. She was sentenced to three years probation, one month in a work release program, and 240 hours of community service. Dare we say, no pain—no gain?

Nighty Night

Now I lay me down to sleep
I hope by morn I'm Meryl Streep
Just my luck all hell will burn
And I'll awake as Howard Stern!

Media Moron of the Millennia Award

No stupid celebrity compilation would be complete without Orenthal James Simpson. After being charged in 1994 with the murders of estranged wife Nicole Brown and her friend Ronald Goldman, Simpson became the target of the slowest police pursuit in history. So laughably slow was the infamous Bronco chase that a dozen women could've given birth to quintuplets. Acquitted in the highly publicized murder trial, the Juice was later found liable in civil court for the wrongful deaths of both Brown and Goldman and ordered to pay over $33 million in damages.

To date, Simpson hasn't paid a penny of the claim. His NFL pension is protected from judgments by California statute, and his home in Florida is equally protected under state law. Simpson has maintained his innocence, and swore that he would spend the rest of his days searching for the true killer of Nicole Brown and Ronald Goldman. True to his word, he has been diligently searching the fairways and clubhouses of golf courses across the country. Anyone see a glove on the thirteenth hole?

Foot in Mouth Award

Rosie O'Donnell is notorious for voicing her opinions, no matter how outrageous they are. In 2007, Ms. Ro went on a conspiracy theory bender during an episode of *The View* regarding the 9/11 tragedy in New York. Apparently taking her cue from a faux documentary "proving" that 9/11 was engineered by the United States' government in order to sway public sentiment into a warlike frenzy, O'Donnell was insistent that structures in New York were intentionally planted with explosives. Despite virtually unanimous professional opinions of leading engineers that the buildings had collapsed due to the weakening of steel supporting structures by intense heat, Ro managed to confuse the concept with the idea that the steel had somehow melted. Structural specialists are firm in their collective opinion that Ms. Ro should stick to penetrating observations about the engineering peculiarities of massive combovers.

WHAT'S ARNOLD SCHWARZENEGGER'S
FAVORITE SEARCH ENGINE?

ALTA VISTA, BABY

Don't Quote Me

Match the lamebrained quote to the moron who uttered it:

a. Corey Feldman   **f.** Anton Chekhov
b. Frank Zappa   **g.** Remy de Gourmont
c. Mick Jagger   **h.** Jimmy Swaggart
d. Justin Timberlake   **i.** Charles Barkley
e. Bryant Gumbel   **j.** Tom Cruise

1. Man is the inventor of stupidity.
2. Sex education classes in our public schools are promoting incest.
3. The stupider the peasant, the better the horse understands him.
4. I love New York City; I've got a gun.
5. I'm more than an actor. I'm an icon, an industry.
6. There is more stupidity than hydrogen in the universe, and it has a longer shelf life.
7. I love kids. I was a kid once, myself.
8. Maybe everybody was coked up, but who cares? It was hot. It was all about sex.
9. I'd rather be dead than singing Satisfaction when I'm forty-five.
10. It's not that I dislike many people. It's just that I don't like many people.

Answers:
1-g, 2-h,
3-f, 4-i, 5-a,
6-b, 7-j, 8-d,
9-c, 10-e

Stupid Says . . .

66This whole Puff Daddy thing has taken a toll on me.**99**

—Sean "Puffy" Combs

Pee Wee's Private Playhouse

Life has been one big legal adventure for comic actor Paul Reubens, better known as Pee Wee Herman. In 1991, the actor instantly killed his career when he was arrested for indecently exposing Pee Wee junior in a Florida adult movie house. He ran afoul of the law again in 2001 after police searched his Los Angeles digs and found what they considered to be a stash of kiddie porn. Prosecutors dropped felony charges after Reubens pled guilty to misdemeanor possession of obscene images which he alleged were part of his "extensive photographic art collection." Yeah, right. And Lindsay Lohan only carries water in her infamous water bottle.

Whoop-Dee-Don't

In 2002, New York radio shock jocks Greg Hughes and Anthony Cumia, popularly known as Opie and Anthony, were overseeing a contest where couples could win a trip by earning points. The only catch was that they had to have sex in a high risk place. The controversy started at Manhattan's St. Patrick's Cathedral when a Virginia couple allegedly engaged in a whoopee session in the vestibule just feet away from worshippers who were celebrating the Feast of the Assumption, a holy day for Roman Catholics. The show's producer was onsite and described the liaison by cell phone. An uproar by Catholic groups and the public followed which resulted in the cancellation of the *Opie and Anthony Show*, and the amorous couple being charged with public lewdness. Whatever happened to just playing *Name that Tune* and winning a toaster?

Diva Darling—Not!

Former New Edition boy bander Bobby Brown has been a tabloid headliner for over a decade after a weirdly dysfunctional marriage to Whitney Houston and numerous brushes with the law. Brown's criminally stupid tendencies surfaced in the media after his arrest for allegedly raping an underage prostitute in 1995 (charges were dropped after he settled out of court), soon after which he was popped again for punching out a Los Angeles hotel security guard. A year later, Brown smashed up Houston's Porsche in Florida, got tagged for drunk driving, and was tossed into the pokey for five days. After volunteering for rehab, Brown showed up drunk for a follow-up visit to the Florida jail and got himself arrested all over again. For the next nine years Brown bounced in and out of jail for parole violations, sexual battery charges, spousal abuse, and assorted idiotic misdemeanors such as urinating on a car belonging to one of Houston's former flames. In February 2007 Brown pulled his ultimate deadbeat dad move when he was arrested for failure to pay over $19,000 in back child support to the mother of two of his four children. Most days, it's just not good *Being Bobby Brown*.

Crustacean Terrorism

In a wacky incident at a Kentucky grocery store in 2004, *Terminator 2* actor Edward Furlong and a few buddies were cracking themselves up by pulling live lobsters from the store tank and playing with them. When police arrived, Furlong added to the insanity by spinning around in circles while one of the officers attempted to frisk him. Irritated, the cops hauled the boozy actor off to the hoosegow to calm down for a few hours while they slapped the seafood simpleton with misdemeanor charges before releasing him. One hopes that several months of rehab was ordered so that Furlong could overcome his propensity for terrorizing innocent crustaceans.

Stupid Says . . .

The difference between Sly Stallone and me is I am me and he is him.
—Arnold Schwarzenegger

Celebudunce Chicanery

Match the lamebrained ignoramus with their idiotic behavior.

a. Arnold Schwarzenegger   **e.** Rush Limbaugh
b. David Hasselhoff   **f.** Mel Gibson
c. Gary Coleman   **g.** Don Imus
d. Bill Clinton   **h.** Paul Ruebens

1. Driving under the influence and spouting off racial slurs at police officers.
2. Got canned after insulting a women's college basketball team.
3. Was arrested for "doctor shopping" as a result of addiction to prescription painkillers.
4. Got caught with his pants down in an adult theater.
5. Was publicly shown on videotape completely sloshed and attempting to eat a hamburger.
6. Was accused by several women of sexual harassment and incidents of groping.
7. Charged with assaulting a woman, and took the case to *People's Court*.
8. Helped some brunette wreck a perfectly good GAP dress.

Answers:
1-f, 2-g,
3-e, 4-h,
5-b, 6-a,
7-c, 8-d

Bumper Snickers!

TELEPATHY HELP WANTED:
YOU KNOW WHERE TO APPLY.
John Edwards

BODY BY NAUTILUS. BRAIN BY MATTEL.
Fabio

Stupid Says . . .

"Researchers have discovered that chocolate produces some of the same reactions in the brain as marijuana. The researchers also discovered other similarities between the two, but can't remember what they are.**"**

—Matt Lauer, host of the Today Show

Slap Happy

Sean Connery, the Scots-born actor who turned James Bond into a household name and one of the most lucrative film franchises in history, created an uproar during a 1987 interview with Barbara Walters. During the gabfest, Connery reiterated comments he'd made over twenty years earlier in a *Playboy* magazine interview that seemed to enhance his long-time image as a ladykiller—one who isn't adverse to slapping women around under the "right circumstances."

"I don't think there's anything wrong with hitting a woman as long as you don't do it the same way you'd hit a man," said 007. And just in case we were all unclear on the subject, he gave further explanation: "An open-handed slap is justified, if all other alternatives fail and there has been plenty of warning." He didn't clarify just what those "alternatives" were, but the statements were appalling by any standard. Odd though it may be, he's been married to Micheline Roquebrune since 1975 without public complaints from her. The truly astonishing thing, however, is that Walters didn't flip him the *Goldfinger*.

Mix and Mingle:
Annoying Celeb Anagrams

a. Charles Barkley
b. Bill Gates
c. Michael Richards
d. O.J. Simpson
e. Don Imus

f. Alec Baldwin
g. Mel Gibson
h. Donald Trump
i. George W. Bush
j. Prince Philip

1. CHEMICAL RASH RID
2. LARD DUMPTON
3. BONG SLIME
4. RICH NIPPLEPI
5. SALARY KERBLECH
6. UNDOISM
7. RUBE EGGSHOW
8. GLIB STEAL
9. BAD CLAWLINE
10. JOINS MOPS

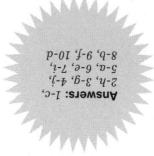

Answers: 1-c,
2-h, 3-g, 4-j,
5-a, 6-e, 7-i,
8-b, 9-f, 10-d

WHY DID PARIS HILTON
DRIVE INTO A DITCH?

TO TURN HER
BLINKER OFF

Bumper Snickers!

THIS BUD'S FOR YOU
Ted Kennedy

IT'S GOOD TO BE THE KING.
Prince Charles

Deep Thoughts

If Moon Unit Zappa started a chain of coffee houses, would they be called Moonbucks?

Stupid Says . . .

"The nice thing about being a celebrity is that when you bore people, they think it's their fault.**"**

—Henry Kissinger